BLOOD RELATIONS

Manfred B. Lee and Frederic Dannay (better known by their joint byline) appear to labor over a manuscript in a publicity photo from the 1940s.

BLOOD RELATIONS

The Selected Letters
Of Ellery Queen
1947-1950

Edited by JOSEPH GOODRICH

With a Foreword by WILLIAM LINK

PERFECT CRIME BOOKS

Contents

foreword

It is an honor to be asked to write a foreword for Joseph Goodrich's fascinating book of letters from the great Ellery Queen and his (their) travails.

As you will learn shortly, if you don't know already, Queen was really two cousins, Fred Dannay and Manfred B. Lee, each brilliant in his own special way. And, two men who couldn't stand each other in their battle for mutual respect. For all you Ellery Queen fans, all you mystery mavens, and all who just like a damn good read, you must sit down and begin enjoying Joseph Goodrich's treasure trove of letters between the Queen cousins, his commentaries and his knowledge of the two men who wrote them. To pique your curiosity, you will be stunned, as was I, with some of the revelations in this book. They are real eye-openers. I will admit that the last few letters almost brought me to tears.

Fred Dannay occupies a very special place in my heart. When my late collaborator Richard Levinson and I were freshmen in college, he published our very first crime story in *Ellery Queen's Mystery Magazine*. The magazine lives and thrives to this day. Our first published story, "Whistling While You Work," started us on a forty-three year journey of writing and producing crime and mystery television shows until Dick's untimely and much lamented death in 1987. I have carried on, especially in the short story genre.

Dick and I were very fortunate to meet Fred and spend a long afternoon talking mysteries with him. We were attending the Mystery Writers of America Edgar Awards dinner in New York City. That evening we won a special Edgar for our *Columbo* and *Ellery Queen* series. We were called to the stage. After receiving our award, I walked from the podium down the steps and saw a salt-and-pepper-bearded older gentleman waiting for us. He embraced me. With a twinkle in his eye, he announced, "I am Ellery Queen." Of course you could have knocked me over even with a snowflake. Dick followed me down and was also embraced warmly.

Here was the surviving member of the great writing team in person. One of our very first mystery idols. We returned to the table where our wives were still applauding (if your wife isn't a fan, you'd better give up!) and sat down, cherishing our Edgars. Soon after, Fred came over and invited us to his home in Larchmont the following day, coincidentally where my sister-in-law Elizabeth resided at the time. Dick and I and our wives quickly cancelled our flight back to Los Angeles, and the two of us took the train from Grand Central Station to meet with Fred.

We were both nervous and excited, anticipating spending the afternoon in the company of this mystery legend. Fred turned out to be a most congenial host and a gracious and chatty gentleman. We were given a late lunch by his very pleasant wife and then we settled down to talk mysteries. The discussion ranged from Fred and Manny's work to other famous mystery writers, both in this country and Europe.

I must explain that Dick and I grew up reading the Queen books and also those of John Dickson Carr. They were our favorites. Carr, a good friend and neighbor of Fred's, was an equal master of creating extremely clever and sometimes incredibly ingenious clues in his fiction. Learning how to create good clues helped us considerably when we created *Columbo*, the biggest hit of our career, where clever but not outrageous clues (we hoped) abounded.

After elementary school classes, we went to school with these three brilliant writers. They were the authors on which we cut our mystery teeth. There was no better training in the world than learning from these extraordinary teachers. Can you imagine these friends Dannay and Carr sitting outside in the warm summer twilight discussing their own work and other greats? Ah, to have been a fly on that garden wall!

I am invariably asked when I lecture at the film schools and universities by the wannabe crime writers, "How do we learn to plot, Mr. Link?" I never tell them what I really believe: the talent for construction is God-given. Instead I tell them to read the best plotters, people like Ellery Queen, John Dickson Carr, Erle Stanley Gardner, Agatha Christie and the new contemporary authors such as Michael Connelly, Jo Nesbo, Don Winslow, and a few others. That's exactly how Dick and I learned when we were young: study the best practitioners and soon you will stop aping them and find a style of your own. But I tell them that virgin writers must write, write, WRITE! Writing must become the most important thing in their lives.

I regret that I didn't have the opportunity to tape our long, delightful, informative afternoon with Fred. I remember that he agreed with us that Carr was one of the true masters. We told him our favorite Queen novel was *Calamity Town*, where the cousins tried to blend a straight novel with the strict detective format. I think they beautifully achieved what they had set out to do. Reread the book and see if you agree. You will be amazed to find how the boys could write out of their hearts and souls as well as their intellects. But I learn now that Fred did not consider *Calamity Town* his personal favorite.

Fred told us something that made both of us very proud. He said that our Ellery Queen series was the best incarnation of the character that had ever been attempted in film or TV. We had written a previous pilot called "Cat of Many Tails." It was changed considerably by the producer while Dick and I were on a trip to Europe. We took our names off the credits and used a *nom de plume*. If you ever see the name Ted Leighton on the screen, I caution you to switch to another channel!

Fred was kind enough not to mention that disaster. Fred liked the lead, Jim Hutton, in our series. We told him that Jim was so committed to the project that he slept at the studio in order to be up early, bushy-tailed, and script memorized for the new shooting day. Now that's a committed actor.

Dick and I had selected the best mystery writers in the film and television field to follow in our fingerprints after we wrote and produced the pilot. Unfortunately we couldn't get a healthy rating with the show. It was scheduled against the extremely popular *Sonny and Cher* series when they reunited after a highly-publicized break-up. The scandal-hungry public was frothing at the mouth to see them back together again. We knew then our series couldn't survive these two mesmerizing stars. It would and did end up in the toilet, a quaint phrase we TV denizens use. We found out later that the man at the helm of NBC programming was not even a mystery fan. Then why the hell had he scheduled the show in the first place?! Welcome to series television, folks.

I still get fan letters and e-mails from people who loved the show. In fact, the series has come out this year in a special boxed set, as Joseph notes. Oh—and one more thing: I forgot to tell you that Fred told us that he came up with all the difficult plots and Manny was the one who fleshed them out and made them novels. This was quite a revelation to us, although we knew all writing teams have different ways of creating mysteries or other fiction.

All this leads to this fine new book by Joseph Goodrich. He knows and loves the Queen *oeuvre* inside out and sideways. I swear he knows even Fred Dannay's shoe size. He has given all of us mystery lovers a great treat by serving up these marvelous letters, showing the joys and tortures of a close, brilliant, wrenching relationship.

I was so astonished to learn of the Queens' vitriolic collaboration. It was the polar opposite of Dick Levinson's and my partnership. We highly respected each other's talent and rarely if ever argued. If we hit a roadblock in our writing, we retired to our families and did our separate thinking. The next morning we met again at our office at Universal and one of us had always come up with the solution. And then we were off and running.

I assumed it was *savant sans dire* that all writing partnerships were at least friendly on the surface. Dick and I were best friends. We grew up together, shared hobbies together and dreamed together. In fact, as our colleague Steve Bochco always said about us—"They even start each other's sentences." In Dick's obituary in *The New York Times*, he stated, "They were more than collaborators, they were brothers." Dick once remarked to me, "I married a woman like you and you married a woman like me." And, indeed he was absolutely correct.

After immersing myself in these letters, I can't believe how the novels ever saw the light of publishing day with all of Fred and Manny's conflicts. But thank the Lord they did! So here's to the Ellery Queen novels, and the reputations of the splendiferous two men who wrote them. These two gentlemen were among the very best.

We all owe a debt of gratitude to Joseph Goodrich who uncovered these gems and who, I am sure, will help bring the intellectual murder mystery back to its former glory. Thanks, Joseph, for what obviously was a labor of love. Your book definitely adds much to the Queen's luster.

WILLIAM LINK
October 2011

William Link and the late Richard Levinson—the "Mr. Rolls and Mr. Royce of American Television" according to *The New York Times*—created, wrote and adapted sixteen on-the-air television series, including *Columbo*, *Murder, She Wrote*, *Mannix*, *McCloud*, and *Ellery Queen*. Link is the recipient of two Emmys, two Golden Globes, a Peabody, the Paddy Chayefsky Laurel Award for Lifetime Achievement in the Art of Television Writing, Four Edgar Allan Poe Awards and the Ellery Queen Award from Mystery Writers of America, the Raymond Chandler Award from the Southern California Chapter of MWA, the Bouchercon XX Mystery Performance Award, and the Agatha Christie Poirot Award—just to name a few. Mr. Link and Mr. Levinson were inducted into the Academy of Television Arts and Sciences Hall of Fame in 1994. An accomplished short story writer whose work frequently appears in *Ellery Queen's Mystery Magazine* and *Alfred Hitchcock's Mystery Magazine*, Link is the author of *The Columbo Collection*, featuring a dozen new Lt. Columbo stories, published by Crippen and Landru.

The ABCs of EQ

From 1928 to 1971, two Brooklyn-born cousins planned and committed hundreds of crimes ranging from theft to blackmail to murder. Instead of being pilloried for their evil-doing, they were world-famous figures heralded for the ingenuity and skill they brought to their careers as mayhem-makers and death-dealers.

I'm not speaking of Mafiosi or members of Murder, Inc. The men I refer to are Frederic Dannay (1905-1982) and Manfred B. Lee (1905-1971), better known by their joint *nom de plume*: Ellery Queen.

Ellery Queen was not one man but two, and the crimes Dannay and Lee committed took place in the pages of books that sold by the millions. As enormously popular mystery writers, they entertained generations of readers; as ambitious and thoughtful authors, their work encompassed the issues and events of over 40 tumultuous years of American—and world—history. A close look at Ellery Queen is a close look at the 20th Century. It is also a look into the psychological workings of two men who created together what neither could create alone.

How did Dannay and Lee come to create Ellery Queen? The story, as related by mystery critics Francis M. Nevins and Jon L. Breen along with others, begins in 1928, when Dannay and Lee were enterprising 23-year-olds working in publicity and advertising—good professions to work in as a decade of noise and hoopla was reaching its height. But these young men had other ambitions. Over lunch on a day in late spring, one of the cousins mentioned an announcement in the *New York Times*: publisher Frederick A. Stokes and *McClure's* magazine were offering a $7,500 award for a new detective novel. This was too good an opportunity for these mystery lovers to pass up. By the time they'd left the restaurant, they'd devised a plot. They worked furiously over the next several months, grabbing an hour here and an hour there, laboring nights and weekends.

Dannay and Lee knew that readers frequently remembered a fictional detective's name but forgot the author's. They decided to give their crime-solver the same name as their pseudonym. But what should that name be? Eventually they hit upon the perfect combination of sound and rhythm. Ellery was drawn from a childhood friend of Dannay's. Queen was chosen because it went well with Ellery. Years later, Dannay explained that he and Lee had been naïve young men and had no idea that Queen meant anything else than a name for royalty.

They finished their manuscript on the final day of the contest, December 31, 1928.

They submitted the book and waited.

And waited.

When they finally worked up the nerve to call the Curtis Brown Literary Agency, which represented both Stokes and *McClure's*, they were told they had won but to keep it under their hats. The results would be made public shortly.

The cousins dreamed of literary fame and tons of money. Why, with $7,500 they could take their wives to the south of France and write one masterpiece after another in delicious exile. They went to Dunhill's and bought pipes, each initialed with *EQ*, to celebrate the start of their new lives as men of letters.

After some time had passed and no word was forthcoming, they called the Curtis Brown Agency again.

Between the first and second call, *McClure's* had gone bankrupt, its assets had been taken over by another magazine, and the new owners had awarded the $7,500 prize to someone else.

"We thought at the time it was a terrible blow from fate," Dannay said many years later. But not all was lost. Frederick A. Stokes published their manuscript as *The Roman Hat Mystery* in 1929, and Ellery Queen, author and detective, was launched.

Dannay and Lee didn't wind up with the prize money. They didn't escape to the south of France to puff on their pipes in a small café. But they got something else, something neither could have foreseen: careers that lasted a lifetime and spanned 39 novels, seven short story collections, innumerable radio plays and reams of critical/editorial musings. Dannay and Lee and their creation grew up together, flourished together—and died together. After Lee's death, Dannay spoke of continuing the series, but nothing came of the idea with the sole exception of "The Reindeer Clue." This slight, pleasant story for the Christmas season, ghosted by Edward D. Hoch, was first published in the *National Enquirer* in 1975. Years later Hoch wrote a few more stories featuring Ellery, and others have tried their hands at it, too. As exercises in nostalgia, these stories are agreeable enough; but the genuine magic perished with the original magicians.

That magic was greatly appreciated in its day. At the height of their popularity in the '40s and '50s, Dannay and Lee were two of the best-known mystery writers in the world. They were profiled in *Life, The New Yorker, Coronet, Publishers Weekly,* and other magazines. Their likenesses were used in an advertisement for Ballantine Ale. You could read Ellery Queen's mystery novels, which sold over 150 million copies in hardcover and paperback. You could see Ralph Bellamy as Ellery in a string of Hollywood B-movies, listen to Ellery's adventures on the radio, and follow his comic book exploits. You could play the Ellery Queen board game, and piece him together as a jigsaw puzzle. Once television came along, Ellery appeared on television, most recently in the 1975-76 NBC series. Dannay and Lee were five-time recipients of the Edgar Award, the Oscar of the mystery genre. They were among the founders of the Mystery Writers of America, which in 1983 created the Ellery Queen Award to honor those in publishing who have made contributions to the genre and to collaborative teams.

Dannay and Lee played a large part in the history and development of the detective story and in 20th Century popular culture. Their novels from the late '20s and early '30s are considered to be classics of the fair-play whodunit. Later work encompassed stylistic experimentation and daring intellectual, social and philosophical content. The post-World-War II novels are particularly audacious, and their scope is wide: mass murder, aberrant psychology, McCarthyism, the passion of Christ, the Death of God, Auschwitz, and the insanity of modern life figure as background and subject. Even the usefulness of reason itself—the cornerstone virtue of the classic mystery—is questioned. Ellery Queen embodies rationality; but what is his role in a world that has been transformed by widespread destruction and genocide? Dannay and Lee were thoughtful men who surveyed the chaos of the world around them. The mystery was the form they used to contain and reflect upon that chaos—a task few other genre writers of the period could have contemplated, much less attempted.

When speaking of Queen's influence, one mustn't forget to mention Dannay's role as editor, anthologist, collector and critic. His four decades at the helm of *Ellery Queen's Mystery Magazine* would be enough to ensure his immortality in mystery publishing. He discovered and supported dozens of new writers and provided a welcoming home for established ones. Add in seminal anthologies such as *101 Years' Entertainment: The Great Detective Stories 1841-1941*, *Rogues' Gallery*, *The Female of the Species* and the multiple volumes of *The Queen's Awards*, and you would still not have fully measured Dannay's accomplishment. He was a fearless proselytizer for the mystery who fought to raise its reputation and secure its legitimacy as a literary form. His work on *EQMM* and the anthologies was a source of contention with Lee, who felt angry and neglected at being left out of the process—a process that he wasn't greatly interested in.

Dannay's editorial activity wasn't the only cause of strife with Lee. Their 40-plus years of collaboration is a history of a competition that had its origins in childhood and was fueled in adulthood by a never-ending need to make a living and support their respective families. Economic catastrophe always threatened; there was rarely a moment of rest for either man. Constant work, constant worry, constant pressure: the freelance writer's lament. These conditions exacted a heavy price on Dannay and Lee. Their relationship—as family, as writers—was dramatic and fractious, composed equally of loving and loathing.

Dannay and Lee were short, balding, bespectacled men who could have been mistaken for dentists or accountants. Their personalities, however, were studies in contrast. Though both were born in Brooklyn, Dannay had an idyllic childhood in a small town in upstate New York, which he recalled with pleasure. Lee was a product of the rough-and-tumble streets of Brownsville, which is still a tough place to grow up, and he once wrote of the emotional withdrawal into literature often made by sensitive Jewish boys to escape the sting of a hostile environment. I believe Lee remained that hurt and injured boy until the day he died. I would bet Dannay—would-be poet, bookworm—made a similar journey inwards for other reasons.

Both were the children of Jewish immigrants, but religion is another dividing point. Dannay was by far the more conventionally religious of the two. His sons made their Bar Mitzvahs, he observed the Jewish High Holidays, and he speaks in one of the letters of how circumstances changed him from a skeptic to a believer. Dannay's life, with its perpetual trials and illnesses—including but not limited to diabetes—was similar at times to Job's. That he found solace in religion is easily understood, and its influence on his imagination ran deep. Neither *Ten Days' Wonder* nor *And on the Eighth Day* would have existed without Dannay's spiritual concerns. One of the most interesting sidelights the letters cast on their work is what Dannay identifies as the essentially Jewish nature of Ellery Queen's character.

Lee's life wasn't far from Job's, either, but his salvation was found in words. His love of language may be his most direct tie to the faith of his forbearers. As biographer and playwright Joan Schenkar once said of Judaism in an interview with Vivian M. Patraka: "It's the only religion I know that enforces literacy (that is, to be bat or bar mitzvahed, you have to be able to read from the Torah), and that exaggerates respect for books (if you drop a sacred text, you're supposed to kiss it)." In all other ways, however, Lee had little time for organized religion.

Lee's ambition was to be the 20th Century's Shakespeare. That he failed to do this is no shame, but the gap between desire and achievement is another source of Lee's torment. And torment it was: "I think my father was one of the unhappiest men I've ever met," said his son Rand. Dannay was committed to the mystery genre, passionate about its history and about its potential. Lee was far less interested in the form *per se*, and conflicted about expending his literary energies on something critics like Edmund Wilson held in contempt. As good as he was at it, he didn't like what he was doing. This highlights yet another difference between the two. Dannay sought to escape his problems by submerging himself in work. Lee was not so lucky; writing the EQ novels, short stories and radio plays offered no escape from his trap—in fact, they *were* the trap.

Dannay was professorial, logical, the one who conceived of and plotted the devilishly clever novels and short stories. His reasonable tone masked a personality that could be easily hurt. Lee was emotional, explosive, and also easily hurt; the one whose gift for character and atmosphere brought the plots to life, creating a fear-choked cityscape as easily as a bucolic New England town. Neither could work without the other, and both chafed against this dependence. Both felt undervalued by the other and anxiously sought the respect and appreciation each felt was his due. Both were bound together emotionally, economically, even legally by Ellery Queen. But the strongest bond of all was familial. "The odds are," one of the cousins told *Look* magazine, "if we were not related by blood we would have separated long ago." Said the other: "I wouldn't put it on that basis. We found ourselves with a valuable property. If we split up, that property would be destroyed."

There was always a pressing need for the money that Ellery Queen generated. The demands on their finances were aggravated by ill health and a series of personal tragedies. Dannay survived a near-fatal car accident in 1940 only to see his first wife die after a protracted battle with cancer, leaving him with two young sons. His second marriage, in other respects a happy one, was troubled with the birth of a severely brain-damaged child who died at the age of six. A third marriage late in life brought Dannay several final years of happiness.

Lee had a much larger family to support—eight children in all, and an ex-wife and various other family members into the bargain. A variety of physical and emotional illnesses plagued his life: high-blood pressure and heart disease, a devastating case of writer's block that lasted for a decade, and a crushing sense of doubt about himself and his work. This is quite apparent in a letter Lee wrote to Dannay on April 15, 1962, just before a hospital stay:

When I look back on my life it seems to me almost non-human in content, in the sense that to be human is to achieve, to rise above oneself, to pull out of life a kind of victory against the odds. I have never been happy, I have never had an instant's peace of mind, I have never known unalloyed pride in myself, I've brought so much pain to those I love to outweigh the few joys I've been able to put into the balance. . . . It makes me angry to think about it—I mean with myself; and I would like the chance to do what I know I have it in me to do— first for myself, and through myself to others, because it can't be done in any other sequence. [. . .]

As we've both said on occasion, you and I are married to each other; and if more often than not it's felt like a marriage made in hell— on both sides—there it is, and neither of us can do anything about the past third of a century. Don't misunderstand me; I'm not crying "*Mea Culpa!*" to sir Galahad. We share the guilt; it takes two to make such a marriage; in our respective weaknesses, psychologically, we needed each other, and perhaps we shall continue to need each other so long as both of us live. But it's an unhealthy need, and I for one would like to live long enough to see the relationship cured of its illness and turned into a healthy one. If, by some remote chance, I don't come out of this, I wanted you to know that.

Lee lived for another nine years, dying of a heart attack in 1971. He was 66 years old. Dannay lived until 1982, but Ellery Queen died with Lee.

For the better part of their careers, Dannay and Lee collaborated at a distance, communicating by letter and telephone. This "geographical separation"—as Dannay wrote on July 2, 1948—was responsible for their "long, involved and perpetually misunderstood letters." Their correspondence bursts with the desire to communicate, to be understood and appreciated by the other. It's also filled with the anger that comes when that desire is frustrated—Lee described one of Dannay's letters as "several thousand words of unfairness and insult and unreasonableness." Dannay was quick to fire back. Only the closeness bred of kinship can explain how they could press each other's sore spots with such accuracy, and to such effect: "This continual buffeting and battering," Dannay wrote in the fall of 1948, ". . . is reducing me to the state where one of these days I won't be able to work *alone*."

Dannay and Lee were notorious for their differences of opinion. "We have basically different attitudes toward the detective story," Dannay once told an interviewer. Lee added, "We have basically different attitudes toward everything." This is borne out by the letters in this volume. Their disagreements were severe, and taken to heart. These letters hurt and gouge, upbraid and lecture and scold. Everything was taken personally and served as a subject of fierce debate, whether it was a possible title, a plot point or the state of the world. It's worth noting that there is a small but distinct element of self-dramatization in all of this. The self being dramatized was, in each case, an unusually sensitive and prickly one. Like Shakespeare's Gloomy Dane, they were predisposed to "the heartaches and the thousand natural shocks that flesh is heir to." Dannay and Lee were passionate, highly neurotic men destined to work together and rile each other for the rest of their lives. "You get sick *after* you open my letters," Lee once wrote to Dannay. "I get sick *before* I open yours. The mere sight of your handwriting on the envelope upsets me."

The cousins were partners in a creative "marriage made in hell," as Lee so astutely phrased it. The division of talent in their collaboration is extreme, and I believe it's a major part of the tension that existed between them. Dannay and Lee were famous for not discussing the way they collaborated, sending up smokescreens whenever the question arose. I speculate that this had to do with shame and anger—the shame they felt about not being able to write alone, anger about being dependent on someone else to start or finish the job. "Each of us jealously guards his individual contribution to the work," Lee wrote in the summer of 1948, "and each resents any encroachment on his work by the other. The mere fact of a disagreement raises instantly an argument or arguments in defense of what is disagreed with."

Francis M. Nevins has suggested that neither Dannay nor Lee could complete a work of fiction alone. If they could have, they certainly would have. Who would go through that much pain if it could be avoided? It couldn't. They needed each other's talent to write the books that paid the bills.

Dannay (with one exception) could conceive of the plot and characters, but couldn't bring those elements to life. Lee (with one exception) could put flesh on the skeleton of a story provided by Dannay, but couldn't come up with the story himself. The exception for Dannay is *The Golden Summer*, a novel based on his Elmira, New York childhood, and published by Little, Brown in 1953. Lee's exception is "The Dauphin's Doll," a short story from 1948 that ranks high among EQ's best shorter works. Lee's ego as a writer resented and resisted being dictated to by Dannay's plots. Dannay felt that Lee considered him nothing more than "a clever contriver" and ran roughshod over his outlines. Dannay was often disillusioned with and disappointed by the finished result. His distaste for *Cat of Many Tails,* for instance, is essentially due to this powerlessness. He must be the only person to have ever felt displeased with *Cat*. It's considered one of their top books, if not the very pinnacle of Queen's accomplishments.

Judging by the letters, their work afforded them little pleasure. Pride, yes; Dannay and Lee were proud of what they wrought. But pleasure seems to be almost entirely lacking, although it wasn't lacking for readers. *Cat* and the other

Queen titles discussed in these letters are enduring works of popular fiction. These vastly ambitious, compulsively readable novels are eminently worthy of being reprinted for new generations of mystery fans.

Francis M. Nevins, who pioneered Queen studies, divides Dannay and Lee's work into four basic periods.

The First Period (1929-1935) contains 13 novels (nine featuring Ellery and his father, Inspector Richard Queen of the NYPD; four novels with the actor Drury Lane, originally published under the pseudonym of Barnaby Ross). These books feature fiendishly complex puzzles and are considered classics of the Golden Age. The Ellery of this period is cast very much in the dandified, super-sleuth mode pioneered by S.S. Van Dine. Ellery is a creature of pure intellect, a Classics-quoting Harvard graduate dressed in flannels and sporting *pince-nez*. Ogden Nash once wrote of Van Dine's detective: "Philo Vance / Needs a kick in the pance." In the opinion of many, this version of EQ could use a good hard boot, as well. "The biggest prig that ever came down the pike," Lee once said of First Period Ellery. Indeed.

The Second Period (1935-1942) contains five novels. It reflects a simplification of the mysteries that Ellery and his father find themselves involved in, and a softening of Ellery's character. Both changes demonstrate Dannay and Lee tailoring their material for the slick magazines and the movies. They achieved some success with the former, and very little with the latter. There has never been a really satisfactory big-screen representation of Ellery Queen. As Nevins says, the novels from this period are intellectually thin and peopled with characters made of the finest—or second-finest—cardboard. In retrospect, these books appear as "a series of steps in the progressive humanization of Ellery and the Queenian universe."

The Third Period (1942-1958) begins with *Calamity Town*, and moves from triumph to triumph over the course of 12 novels. Nevins writes:

> In this period there was nothing Queen would not dare. We find complex deductive puzzles; achingly full-drawn characterizations; the detailed evocation of a small town and a great city, each of which comes to life on the page; the creation of a private, topsy-turvy Alice-in-Wonderland otherworld; explorations into the historical, psychiatric and religious dimensions; hymns of hate directed at McCarthyism and other brands of political filth; a gently sketched middle-age love story; a nostalgic re-creation of Ellery's young manhood.

The novels and short stories of this period are rich with invention and feeling. They came at the cost of the health and peace-of-mind of their creators, as the letters indicate, but the reader can only be thankful that the price was paid. The work of Period Three is the summit of Dannay and Lee's creative life.

The Fourth Period (1963-1971) includes nine novels and follows a five-year hiatus. This break is generally ascribed to Lee's writer's block and to a desire on the part of the cousins to bring the Queen saga to an end. Given Dannay and Lee's dependence on Queen for their livelihood, I've always wondered about this conclusion. Were they really thinking about abandoning Ellery? Perhaps a better question is what convinced them to bring Ellery back in *The Player on the Other Side*. No definitive answer to this question exists. We do know that Lee was still suffering from writer's block and that Theodore Sturgeon did the initial work on the book. Lee conquered his writer's block and wrote the last several EQs, including the non-Ellery stand-alone *Cop Out*. This novel, with its contemporary setting and vulgar, low-rent characters, is unlike anything else the cousins ever attempted, and is underrated because of that.

According to Nevins, the novels of the fourth and last period recycle motifs from previous periods and exemplify Dannay's interest in overtly artificial puzzle-making. There is a withdrawal from the contemporary scene, "a retreat from attempts at naturalistic plausibility." One might call it EQ's mannerist period, of great interest to devotees but, perhaps, less intriguing to others. Though none of these last books scale the heights of previous work, there is a great deal in them for the Queen fan to appreciate.

The contents of *Blood Relations* were culled from the Frederic Dannay Papers which are housed in the Rare Book and Manuscript Library, Columbia University, New York City. Columbia acquired the Papers from Dannay's sons Douglas and Richard in the 1980s. The majority of the letters are drawn from 1947-50, Manfred B. Lee's years in North Hollywood. Very little material before or after those years has survived.

Choosing what to include and what to leave out was a difficult task. I've focused on material that casts new light on the novels, the collaboration that produced them, and the personal lives of the collaborators. There are gaps in the correspondence; the letters offer a fascinating if fragmentary look at Dannay and Lee during their peak creative years. We are granted a view of the cousins at work during the middle of their third and most productive period (1942-1958). The letters document aspects of the creation of *Ten Days' Wonder*, *Cat of Many Tails* and *The Origin of Evil*, all of which are ranked among the very best of the Queen *oeuvre*.

As someone who has been reading Ellery Queen for over 30 years, I found this collection a pleasure to assemble and edit. I come away from the work with a much greater sense of what those two talented, flawed, sensitive men must have been like. My admiration for Ellery Queen has been enormous since I first started reading him. My admiration for these cousins from Brooklyn increased with each letter I read. Gods alone create with ease; men must struggle. Dannay and Lee struggled, and succeeded. It cost them greatly, however, and these letters document a portion of that struggle and its cost.

My hope is that the reader will hear Dannay and Lee as they debate, discuss, argue and commiserate. I have tried to stay out of their way, providing contextual material and commentary only when necessary or appropriate.

An ellipsis in brackets—[. . .]—indicates that I have cut material which is redundant or not germane. Dannay and Lee were given to quoting each other's letters as well as their own in service of a point, and I have cut a great deal of their extensive reiterations and repetitions while doing my best not to distort the tone or meaning of the letters.

Three asterisks (* * *) used to divide sections of the letters indicate divisions originally made by Dannay and Lee.

Dannay's half of the correspondence is mainly composed of copies; the originals were sent to Lee. Very few of these copies are signed. For the sake of clarity, I have appended Dannay's standard signature ("Dan") to these copies. Book titles have been italicized, as has underlining in this mostly typewritten correspondence. A few spelling and typographical errors have been corrected.

A warning: What follows contains spoilers. Plots are revealed. Killers are named.

JOSEPH GOODRICH
Brooklyn, N.Y.
October 2011

A Queen Chronology

1905: Emanuel Benjamin Lepofsky (Manfred B. Lee) born in Brooklyn, N.Y. on January 11.
Daniel Nathan (Fred Dannay) born in Brooklyn, N.Y. on October 20.
1906: The Nathan family moves to Elmira, N.Y.
1917: The Nathan family returns to New York City.
1925: Lee graduates from New York University.
1926: Dannay marries Mary Beck.
1927: Lee marries Betty Miller.
1929: *The Roman Hat Mystery* is published by Fredrick A. Stokes.
1930: *The French Powder Mystery* (Stokes).
1931: *The Dutch Shoe Mystery* (Stokes).
1932: *The Greek Coffin Mystery* (Stokes).
The Egyptian Cross Mystery (Stokes).
The Tragedy of X and *The Tragedy of Y* (under the Barnaby Ross pseudonym) are published by Viking.
1933: *The American Gun Mystery* (Stokes).
The Siamese Twin Mystery (Stokes).
The Tragedy of Z and *Drury Lane's Last Case* (under the Barnaby Ross pseudonym), Viking.
Douglas Dannay is born.

Jacquelin Lee is born.

Anya Peter Lee is born. (Lee adopts her after he marries her mother, Kaye Brinker in 1942.)

1934: *The Chinese Orange Mystery* (Stokes).
The Adventures of Ellery Queen (Stokes).

1935: *The Spanish Cape Mystery* (Stokes).
Patricia Lee is born.

1936: *Halfway House* (Stokes).
Danger: Men Working, EQ's only stage play (written in collaboration with Lowell Brentano), plays a handful of performances in Baltimore and Philadelphia but never makes it to New York City.
Publishers Weekly article reveals that Dannay and Lee are "Ellery Queen."

1937: *The Door Between* (Stokes).

1938: *The Four of Hearts* (Stokes).
Lee and his wife Betty Miller separate.

1939: *The Dragon's Teeth* (Stokes).
The Adventures of Ellery Queen makes its radio debut. Over the next nine years it will move from CBS to NBC to ABC, change casts, time slots and sponsors, but still maintain a following.
Richard Dannay is born.

1940: *The New Adventures of Ellery Queen* (Stokes).
Dannay is seriously injured in an automobile accident.

1941: *101 Years' Entertainment: The Great Detective Stories, 1841-1941* (Little, Brown).
Ellery Queen's Mystery Magazine debuts.
Lee and Betty Miller divorce.

1942: *Calamity Town* (Little, Brown).
The Detective Short Story: A Bibliography (Little, Brown).
Lee marries Catherine Fox ("Kaye") Brinker.

1943: *There Was an Old Woman* (Little, Brown).
Christopher Rebecca ("Kit") Lee is born.

1945: *The Murderer Is a Fox* (Little, Brown).
The Casebook of Ellery Queen (Mercury Bestseller).
Anthony Joseph Lee is born (died 1987).
Mary Dannay dies.

1947: Manfred B. Lee, Jr. is born.
Lee moves from Norwalk, Connecticut to North Hollywood, California to supervise the EQ radio show.
Dannay marries Hilda Wiesenthal, and the Dannays move to Larchmont, N.Y.

1948: *Ten Days' Wonder* (Little, Brown).
Stephen Dannay is born.
EQ radio show ends its run.
1949: *Cat of Many Tails* (Little, Brown).
1950: *Double, Double* (Little, Brown).
Lee and family return to the East Coast, moving to Westport, Connecticut, then to Roxbury.
1951: *The Origin of Evil* (Little, Brown).
Queen's Quorum: A History of the Detective-Crime Short Story As Revealed By The 100 Most important Books Published In This Field Since 1845 (Little, Brown).
Rand Benjamin Lee born.
1952: *The King Is Dead* and *Calendar of Crime* (Little, Brown).
1953: *The Scarlet Letters* (Little, Brown).
1954: *The Glass Village* (Little, Brown).
Jeffrey Robert Lee is born (died 1990).
Stephen Dannay dies at the age of six.
1955: *QBI: Queen's Bureau of Investigation* (Little, Brown).
1956: *Inspector Queen's Own Case* (Simon & Schuster).
1957: *In the Queen's Parlor, And Other Leaves from the Editors' Notebook* (Simon & Schuster).
1958: *The Finishing Stroke* (Simon & Schuster).
1963: *The Player on the Other Side* (Random House).
1964: *And On the Eighth Day* (Random House).
1965: *The Fourth Side of the Triangle* and *Queen's Full* (Random House).
1966: *A Study in Terror* (Lancer).
1967: *Face to Face* (New American Library).
1968: *The House of Brass* (New American Library).
QED: Queen's Experiments in Detection (New American Library).
1969: *Cop Out* (The World Publishing Company).
1970: *The Last Woman in his Life* (World Publishing Company).
1971: *A Fine and Private Place* (World Publishing Company).
Manfred B. Lee dies at the age of 66 on April 3.
1972: Hilda Dannay dies.
1975: Levinson and Link's *Ellery Queen* TV series debuts and lasts for one season.
"The Reindeer Clue" is published in the *National Enquirer*.
Dannay marries Rose Koppel.
1982: Frederic Dannay dies at the age of 76 on September 3.

1947: Ten Days' Wondering

In October 1947, Fred Dannay and his second wife Hilda (known as "Bill") are living in Larchmont, N.Y. Fourteen-year-old Douglas and eight-old Richard—Dannay's sons from his first marriage—live with them. Dannay is about to celebrate his forty-second birthday, and there's cause for celebration: Hilda is pregnant.

Manfred B. Lee turned 42 in January. He and his second wife Kaye and their three children—four-year-old Kit, two-year-old Tony and the infant Manfred, Jr.—live in North Hollywood. Lee moved from Connecticut to California to write and supervise *The Adventures of Ellery Queen* radio show. Lee is performing his usual task in the collaboration, the actual writing; but the plots for the show have been provided by others for the last few years. The demands of *Ellery Queen's Mystery Magazine* and his first wife's death in 1945 led Dannay to leave active work on the show. His function has been filled by critic and mystery novelist Anthony Boucher and radio writer Tom Everitt.

Otherwise, Dannay's life follows the pattern established in 1941: He devises the plots for the EQ novels and stories, edits *Ellery Queen's Mystery Magazine* and supervises its yearly short story contest. He is a quiet and unassuming man; his neighbors in Larchmont have little idea that he's one-half of a celebrated writing team.

The radio program, like the magazine, is a steady and welcome source of income. Or perhaps not so steady, as it turns out: *The Adventures of Ellery Queen* lost its sponsor in late September and would not return to the air until the end of November as a sustaining (i.e., unsponsored) program.

The cousins are on opposite coasts, collaborating at a distance. A regular letter, delivered by train, is too slow, so they keep the U.S. Postal system hopping with frequent (and lengthy) airmail specials. Less frequently, they communicate by telephone; making a long-distance call was an expensive and time-consuming process in those days.

There's a lot to discuss. Lee has just received the outline for a new novel that Dannay calls *Ten Days' Wonder*.

The outline is for the third Queen novel set in the small New England town of Wrightsville. (The first was 1942's *Calamity Town*, the second 1945's *The Murderer Is a Fox*.) In the outline, Howard Van Horn, an acquaintance from Ellery's days in pre-war Paris, comes to Queen for help. Howard suffers from periodic blackouts, and he is afraid of what he might do in an amnesiac state. Can Ellery help him? Ellery doesn't think so; he's not a psychiatrist, and it's clear that professional assistance is what's really needed. But Ellery can't refuse the troubled young man's request. He accompanies Howard to the Van Horn estate in the ritziest part of Wrightsville.

There EQ meets Sally, Howard's attractive young stepmother; the lean and cynical Wolfert, Howard's uncle; and Christina, Howard's ancient and religiously obsessed grandmother. Towering over them all is Howard's father, Diedrich Van Horn. Diedrich is a titan of a man, built on a massive scale, a dominant and domineering force.

Ellery learns that Howard and Sally are having an affair. Incriminating letters have been stolen, and the lovers are being blackmailed. Against his better judgment, Ellery tries to help. Matters deteriorate quickly. Ellery's attempts backfire and he leaves the Van Horn estate in disgrace. A flash of insight reveals the pattern behind the events at the Van Horns'. The Ten Commandments are being systematically violated—and Howard is behind it. When Ellery realizes that "Thou Shalt Not Kill" is the only unbroken Commandment, he knows that Howard intends to murder his father. Ellery hurries back to the Van Horns' but arrives too late. Howard has strangled Sally, who had been asleep in Diedrich Van Horn's bed. Having mistakenly killed the woman he loved, unable to face the upcoming murder trial, Howard commits suicide. He slits his wrists, puts his head in a noose, then blows his brains out. The case is brought to a horrific conclusion.

Almost a year later, Ellery's discovery of a stray bit of information leads him to the conclusion that Howard was not actually guilty. Diedrich Van Horn was the blackmailer and the strangler who, drawing upon the hell-and-brimstone religion of his youth, chose the Ten Commandments as the substructure for his revenge. Howard and Sally committed adultery, Diedrich Van Horn made sure that Howard appeared to have broken the other nine Commandments, as well . . . including murder. A fan of Queen's novels, Diedrich knew that this plan was catnip for someone like Ellery—and that it would lead him to the wrong conclusion. Ellery has been as easily worked upon as poor Howard.

Ten Days' Wonder is the best of Queen's novels. Powerful, darkly elegant, *Wonder* possesses a sharpness and a bleak clarity that only a handful of the other EQs share. Its complicated plot is marked by Dannay's taste for God-like manipulators, and it is not marred by his taste for the self-conscious and self-referential fun-and-games that weaken the later books. Its conception has scale and grandeur, mixing, in Nevins's phrase, "crime fiction with cosmic drama."

Lee's prose rises to the occasion and is almost entirely free of the rhetorical flourishes that contemporary readers may find hard to take in other Queen novels. What heightened language *Wonder* contains is justified by the way it echoes the language of the King James Bible—the source of the book's concept.

The maturity and depth of the characterizations are another aspect of *Wonder*'s strength. We view Howard and Sally sympathetically but are appalled when they betray Ellery. We see how fallible they are, and how terribly people can behave. We feel for them and for Ellery—most of all for Ellery, because he was only trying to help.

He didn't succeed. His failure is all the more galling as his own methods were used against him. Ellery's much-vaunted logic has proved to be nothing more than a means by which he may be manipulated. His appetite for the complicated and *outré* was the bait on the hook.

When his methods fail him, so does the possibility of conventional punishment. Here is where *Ten Days' Wonder* really gets shocking. Ellery Queen, master detective, son of a police Inspector, bypasses the law and takes matters into his own hands by giving Diedrich Van Horn two choices: Exposure . . . or the gun in the desk drawer.

A shot rings out as Ellery leaves the Van Horn estate and walks into the darkest of nights.

The pillars of Ellery's life—the rational detection of crime and its legal punishment—have been toppled. He walks away a shaken and sorrowful man. It is no surprise that Dannay conceived of *Ten Days' Wonder* as Ellery's last case.

This was a source of controversy with Lee, as was almost everything concerning Ellery, who seems to have been regarded more as an actual son than a fictional character. Unfortunately, the letter in which Dannay broaches this idea is missing, and all we have is his response to what must have been Lee's very great surprise. End Ellery's career? Impossible! But that is exactly what

Dannay is suggesting. He thought deeply about the nature of Ellery's character, and how it should—how it *must*—change with the times . . . even to the point of bringing Ellery's years of detection to a close. But Lee had his own ideas and was more than willing to fight for them.

Dannay mentions his desire to give *Wonder* "a magazine fling". Publication in one of the well-paying, mass-market magazines of the era such as *The Saturday Evening Post* or *Collier's* was highly desirable—and elusive. Ellery hadn't appeared in one of the slicks since 1938, when *Cosmopolitan* published *The Four of Hearts*. That was EQ's last outing in the glossies until *Redbook* published *The House of Brass* in 1968.

There were no takers for *Ten Days' Wonder*. In retrospect, this is not hard to understand. It is a bleak novel that signally fails to do what magazine literature must: Reassure us that, no matter what little troubles may come to us, all is well. All is decidedly *not* well in *Ten Days' Wonder*. Lives have been lost and a vocation abandoned. The taste of ashes is inescapable.

The question of a sale to the slicks—and what constitutes a manuscript that the slicks would want to buy—is a source of hot and angry debate over the next book, *Cat of Many Tails*.

But it is not the only source of contention. It never was. We begin with two letters from Dannay.

October 18, 1947

Dear Man:

Herewith a 59-page outline of the new Queen novel, *Ten Days' Wonder*; also some additional notes, references, etc.

It represents, after the abandonment of my first attempt, two months of solid, grueling work, with the fluorescent lights in my study on many a night. I hit a peak one night by working until 3:00 a.m. I've reached the point where I've got a bellyful of *Ten Days' Wonder*, and will be glad to see it out of my hands and into yours.

I hope you like it.

I'm going to take it easy for a couple of days, then I must get back to work again. Here is my schedule, which I feel you should know.

1. This year's contest ends October 20th. We shall probably have about 700 manuscripts. Of course, they all pass through readers at the magazine office first, but I will still have plenty of manuscripts to read before the contest can be closed out. Then I have to decide on the prize winners, prepare the prize-winning stories for publication—say, about 15, at least. Also, prepare the stories for book-anthology (although we have no contract as yet). All this is a long, brutal job.

2. I have to prepare two issues of the magazine almost immediately. I had prepared the magazine well in advance, so that I could work on the novel with a minimum of interruptions, but this advance work has now been eaten up.

3. I have to edit and put together the last of the Dashiell Hammett books of shorts, including an introduction.

4. I have to put together the O. Henry book, including an introduction.

All this must be finished by January 1st —so you see I've still got my work cut out for me. I'll have all I can do to finish by the first of the year.

Should the radio situation not develop into our being on the air soon, I suggest that you dig into the novel full time. If the radio show goes back on the air, I suggest that you arrange your work so that whatever part of the week you can possibly spare is put into the novel just as religiously as you can manage it. Work out the time factors as best you can and let me know approximately when you think the novel might be finished (a) without the radio show to do, and (b) with the radio show back on the air. The reason I ask this is important: I will be free again beginning the first of the year, or thereabouts; it would be wise for us to plan ahead, so that I know what it will be best for me to do.

At this precise moment I cannot think in terms of another novel; yet it may be necessary for me to start on another novel after the first of the year.

Remember, too, that we shall want to give the new novel a magazine fling. This usually takes a good two months. Little, Brown would want to publish no later than the Winter of 1948—unless a magazine sale simply forces them to delay book publication. But you know the difficulties of book production today— Little, Brown would need an absolute minimum of six months for the mechanical end alone. Naturally, too, the more time available for possible magazine sale, the better.

Think it all over, and let me know your estimates, opinions, etc.

About *Ten Days' Wonder*: The outline herewith is the first draft from notes. I expected to do another draft, polishing, tightening, and so on, as might be needed. But I don't think enough would be gained by taking the time to do a second draft—and as I've already indicated, I haven't the stamina to start over again. I'm just knocked out. Bear in mind, this is the first sustained full-length job I've done in a long time, and I did it under harrowing circumstances—ill health, rustiness, self-doubts.

I can only repeat: I hope you like it.

DAN

Dannay and Lee discussed the treatment by telephone, and that discussion prompted the next two letters.

October 24, 1947

Dear Man:

[. . .] First, some of your specific criticisms or questions, as I remember them. Why Wrightsville? Why not? A Wrightsville story does not mean that the story has to be a town treatment, like *Calamity Town*. *The Murderer Is a Fox* treated Wrightsville from the viewpoint of a single family. The new novel does virtually the same. There is no absolute necessity, merely because the story is laid in Wrightsville, to bring in all the town. The Van Horn household also represents a slice of American life—different from the Foxes and the Haights, but that is as it should be. Wrightsville novels should be different from one another.

I see concrete advantages in using Wrightsville, even as a background and no more. It means the new book will be the third in a series—the saga of Wrightsville is growing. I can even foresee a possible omnibus of the three Wrightsville cases, with a special title. Two are not enough to give a series effect; but three begins to mean "saga." Besides, there are no *dis*advantages.

I see each of the Wrightsville novels as revealing a slice of American life, but a different slice in each book. The Van Horns represent the rich slice, with gentility, a veneer of culture, a civilized exterior, the refinement of wealth. Surely this is America too—and what's inside? Twisted lives, tragedy—and moral rottenness. That's one part of Wrightsville, as Wrightsville is one part of America.

Why Ellery's last case? Is it possible you have missed a point here? The new novel is in part an exposure of detective novels and of fictional detectives; even more relevant and important, it is an exposure of Ellery, as a character and as a detective. The exposure is complete and devastating, with the satirical finish that in the end he is still right. But in the process of this exposure, and as a result of it, Ellery should emerge as a human being. In my opinion the only logical conclusion of the total exposure of Ellery's fallibility and "brilliance" is that he gives up detection. Hence, his last case.

The characters of Wolfert and Christina: I disagree that these characters are either unnecessary or unintegrated in the present version. They are both important, especially psychologically. True, the novel is the story of three people—Diedrich, Howard, and Sally—seen through the eyes of Ellery (in the present version). The other characters are secondary. But secondary characters are not unnecessary merely because they are admittedly secondary; nor do secondary characters have to appear in all scenes to be fully integrated. Christina especially plays a very important part: psychologically, she prepares the way for the Biblical theme. And both Christina and Wolfert add a certain fullness to the feeling of human beings in a large house. Their purpose from a detective story standpoint is also there, but not important enough to discuss.

Which brings me to your general reaction: you said that you found parts of the story "pedestrian." This puzzles me, but good. Just what do you mean by pedestrian? Do you mean that the events of the story are commonplace, everydayish? Do you mean that a blackmail situation is *per se* pedestrian? Or that thefts of jewels and a love-triangle are *per se* pedestrian? If that is what you mean, again I have the feeling that you have missed the point. Either that, or as of old, we simply do not eye things the same way.

The basic theme of the new book is the Ten Commandment crimes. If that is pedestrian, then I give up: I cannot believe that you meant the Ten Commandments theme as pedestrian—you must have meant the *developing* events, incidents, and situations. The Ten Commandments theme, in my opinion, is sensational material, spectacular to the point of verging on fantasy. If anything, it is too sensational.

Now, if the Ten Commandments theme were surrounded by equally spectacular material, it would run the whole business into the ground; it would be overdone; it would become fantastic, even bizarre. But if the Ten Commandments theme is surrounded deliberately—and I repeat, deliberately—with seemingly commonplace events, two tremendous things result: first, the what-you-call pedestrian development protects and emphasizes the true contrast values inherent in the Ten Commandments theme; and second, the everyday events make the Ten Commandments theme believable, credible, realistic. For if the Ten Commandments theme can arise out of commonplace situations, then it could happen, and if it could happen, it is realistic. Conversely, just for the sake of clarity in this letter, if the Ten Commandments theme stemmed from out-of-the-ordinary events, then it would seem as if the Ten Commandments theme were possible *only* if out-of-the-ordinary events occurred to make it possible.

The seemingly everydayish quality of the build-up and development, far from being pedestrian in an adverse way, is so highly desirable in this story that, in my opinion, it is utterly unavoidable. Any other type of treatment would lead inevitably to incredibility—which in this book would be fatal. [. . .]

All our best. Bill is feeling very well—no morning sickness, or discomfort. I hope her pregnancy continues to be free from the discomforts most women have. The boys are well too. The only one in the house who "crechxes" [sic] (there's a word!) is yours truly, but I found the grind on the novel extremely wearing, and I'm tired, and I face a hell of a lot of past-due work to clean up, and generally have some excuse for feeling pooped. Take that damn contest, for example: Each year the contest is a life-saver for the magazine, but here this year's contest is officially closed and I have no semblance of a $3000 first-prize winner! I wake up in the middle of the night and find myself wondering what in the world I'm going to do. There are still some manuscripts by VIPs coming in—at least, they've been promised—and I'm pinning my waning hopes on these last-ones-in. And you think you have troubles!

DAN

Oct. 25 [1947]. Saturday night.

Dear Dan:

[. . .] I chose a bad word in "pedestrian"—I understood why you picked commonplace incidents, etc., although I disagree with you as to their impact in the whole structure: they can't possibly seem other than commonplace incidents *until* the Ten Commandments thing comes out, and by then most of the book is under the reader's belt. The question is, how will they "read" until that point is reached? However, this was not my major concern—in my haste, I failed to make myself clear. What I really meant, and what really bothered me, was that some of the incidents were strongly reminiscent of *Calamity Town* and Jim Haight. Being set in Wrightsville, the reminiscence is only enhanced. I'm afraid of a certain quality of sameness in development (which, admittedly, is lost in the shuffle when the dénouement is revealed) . . . As for my criticism of the brother and mother as being unnecessary characters, I see your point about the old lady as being a preparation for the upshot, but I don't see the place of the brother at all. Unless I missed something, he seemed to me unintegrated. That is, there is no "material" on him. I shall have to manufacture some in the sense of a bystander—develop character rather than incident, that is, where he is concerned. And that's tough in a mystery where too much revealed about a character threatens to upset the psychological balance of the structure.

This, however, is all quite literally fruitless, judging by our past experiences. I think it much better all around if we engage in no further punting duel over it. I'll do the novel substantially along the lines of the present outline; I say "substantially" because I'm sure you will grant me the leeway implicit in any writing job, where new factors creep in or things assume new proportions in the writing.

Not to belabor this, in view of my last paragraph, but before we close the chapter on these novel discussions, I need your further explanations on one important point. How do you see Howard, or rather how did you see him in planning this? To me he is an enigma, viewed in the ordinary light. For instance, I don't understand his attitude toward Ellery when Ellery wouldn't keep his mouth shut. He goes into "an almost insane tantrum," upbraiding Ellery "violently" for having "committed the greater offense," etc. For most of the story until that point, Howard had seemed to me a pretty decent sort—at least, that's what I thought you had in mind for him. Now he suddenly turns rat—not only rat, but a rat with a ridiculous sense, certainly unjustified by any sane standard, of injury. He was willing to let Ellery take an unjustified rap for him and Sally—and that I don't understand in view of his previous characterization. Then, on top of this, he gets sore because Ellery refuses to take the unjustified tap! This is the hallmark of an unbalanced mind. Is that what you meant to convey? I can handle him easily enough as a disturbed character, irrational, etc.; but even irrationality has to have something to back it up, and if it's there I didn't get it on an admittedly hasty reading. Granted that he is disturbed about his attacks of blackout, is this enough to motivate his unreasonable, selfish, really stupid attitude toward Ellery? I should have thought you wanted Howard to get reader sympathy; believe me, no matter what the buildup, the reader will drop him like a hot potato when he lashes out at Ellery, "insane tantrum" or not. On the other hand, if Howard is sane, I'd like to know him a bit better than the outline reveals him. This is obviously important and, busy as you are, warrants a letter of character amplification. Maybe I've missed the boat on him somewhere; if so, set me on the course.

You asked me in the letter attached to the outline when I could expect to get the novel finished. With the radio show to be done, I would shoot for March 1st. Whether I can make that date or not depends on many factors. Certainly I will do my best to make that date or better it. [. . .]

We are still not settled here. The problems are great, and progress difficult. One of these happy years we'll be normal.

Kaye and I were both happy to hear that Bill's pregnancy is going along so well, and Kaye especially sends Bill her love. Our kids are fine—the baby is gaining remarkably—now weighs almost 18 pounds—he's gained I think it's 6 pounds since we got here! Tony's nose shows no improvement, and we have an appointment with a big nose specialist for a week from Monday. It will undoubtedly mean an operation, something we don't look forward to, believe me. But the poor little guy needs help. If you heard him breathe on some nights, you'd understand why we're willing to risk a great deal to give him relief. Kit is wonderful—big and golden-brown. They all love it here. The weather, after a short cool spell, has turned warm again; the sun shines all day; it's good after those damned humid or cold spells back East [. . .]

Regards,

MANNY

Dannay refers in the following letter to the "Shakespearian fillip"—the sense of confirmation and rightness—these lines from Henry VI, 3.ii impart to the structure of the book:

> RICHARD III: *That would be ten days' wonder at the least.*
> GEORGE PLANTAGENET: *That's a day longer than a wonder lasts.*

Ellery is something of a nine days' wonder in the novel. His stunning solution to the case is shown on the tenth day to have been—crushingly, fatally—wrong.

Dannay's letter also contains much concrete advice on mystery writing. In justifying his choices to Lee, he explains how he made them: how the action of this book is dependent on its generative idea—the Ten Commandments; and how a reader's suspicions can be anticipated and distributed among a novel's characters. Dannay must have been a wonderful teacher the few times he ventured into the halls of academe. Also of note is the way he compares and contrasts *Ten Days' Wonder*'s use of Wrightsville with *Calamity Town*, Ellery's first visit to that small town nestled in the shadows of a New England mountain range.

October 29, 1947

Dear Man:

[. . .] True, the commonplace incidents will not take on their full meaning until the Ten Commandments theme comes out; but I don't see this as too adverse a criticism. There is one tremendous advantage in seemingly everydayish events; they will have the smack of reality, without stretching for effects, and you can capitalize on this substance of realism. Also, the actual events, while commonplace, are not so commonplace that they are without interest. Naturally, it is only my own opinion, but I think what happens to Howard, Sally and Ellery will hold the readers' interest: mood, pressure, the growth of tension, the inevitability of tragedy, and something else too that I think you can get into the story: the feeling, which will also grow as the story progresses, that there *is* something behind all this, something that eludes Ellery and the reader and yet manifests itself in the tension and in the terrible pressure from the outside. I think also that we can assume that Queen fans, real Queen fans and real detective story fans, will be looking for that "extra" that Queen books have always had; naturally, you cannot depend on this expectancy, but you can *incite* it; you can subtly prepare the reader for it. Actually, the very commonplaceness should "read" well—if you achieve the suspense that is inherent in the situation and in the mood.

I was aware of a certain reminiscent quality which seemed to tie *Ten Days' Wonder* to *Calamity Town*. I considered this very carefully, and for better or for worse decided that the similarity was not strong enough to be a deterrent. The only real similarity is that there was a blackmail and pawning-of-jewelry thread in *Calamity Town*. But that's all they were: threads. They were not an important part of the story of *Calamity Town*; they came out only as evidence at the trial and they were explained briefly in the end. But the big thing is that in *Calamity Town* these threads were hidden, secret; they came out into the open only as passing explanations at the very end. In *Ten Days' Wonder* the blackmail and pawning of jewelry are in the open; their mechanics are exposed to the reader; they are dealt with as important matters of plot. The reader sees them happen, with a significance altogether different from that in *Calamity Town*. Further, there will be at least five years between *Calamity Town* and *Ten Days' Wonder*; and further still, *Calamity Town* never had any magazine publication whatever.

I don't really think there is any quality of sameness, as you express it, in the development of the two stories. The big events and the larger situations are not alike at all, and the *significance* of the events in *Ten Days' Wonder* is as far removed from *Calamity Town* as any two basic ideas could possibly be. Don't underestimate the tremendous difference between treating, say, a blackmail theme secretly on the one hand, and openly on the other.

Perhaps I should point this out too: if you don't already realize it, you will become more and more aware, as you soak in the story, that certain plot ideas are not merely devices. The basic situation in *Ten Days' Wonder*, once you accept the Ten Commandments theme, is utterly and completely unavoidable. The basic situation that concerns Howard, Sally, and Diedrich is not picked out of thin air; it is not a matter of selection. It is inevitable. In order to develop the Ten Commandments theme, it is absolutely *necessary* for Howard to be guilty of two crimes: he *must* covet Diedrich's wife and he *must* have committed adultery. Howard's guilt in breaking these two Commandments is the fulcrum of the story; on this hinges everything—the development of the other eight crimes, even the very solution itself. If you reread the last part of the novel (I mean, the tenth chapter), you will understand even more clearly that the vital point in the story, the crux of Ellery's solution, is based on and stems from the inescapable essential that Howard covets Sally and is guilty of adultery.

With such an absolute "must" the construction and development of the story is not a matter of my whim of selection. I had to follow through, logically, inevitably. And surely this inevitability of material, even though in minor respects it reminds you of *Calamity Town*, is a highly desirable kind of development—especially in a detective story.

I don't know if you see this as clearly as I do—but you will, as the story digs deeper and deeper into you. I'd like very much for you to study this angle and let me know if the inevitability in the choice of *basic* material makes itself more and more impressive. The Ten Commandments theme *must* evolve from a sex (love) triangle: this dictates the development.

Before I forget: you did not comment on the title of the book and the unusual way in which the title gives the book its specific form. How do you like the title, the break-up of nine-days'-wonder and the denouement of a tenth-day-wonder? How do you like the sheer pattern in the very form which the book takes physically? Of course, the Shakespearian fillip to the division of a ten days' wonder into two parts of nine days and a tenth day is sheer luck; the very perfection of it, I admit, influenced me—in the sense that I had the unshakable conviction that this was it, that even Shakespeare was on our side. Of course, I had the form, the break-up of nine days and a final, devastating tenth day, *before* I discovered Shakespeare—it was a sort of inspirational confirmation to find in Shakespeare such extraordinary appositeness.

Now, as to Diedrich's brother, Wolfert: far from being unintegrated, Wolfert is integrated with considerable subtlety. I'll try to explain. I should say, here, that I am writing these thoughts and explanations off the cuff, ad lib so to speak, and I have the overwhelming fear of the futility of words. All these matters seem so clear to me, yet I am plagued by the feeling that I am not getting them over to you. But I'll try my best.

Wolfert serves a function comparable to that of the old lady's. You now see that the old lady is a psychological "plant"—she prepares the way for the acceptance of the Biblical theme, she subtly sets the stage for the big surprise, the big shock. Okay. Wolfert is also a psychological plant. He takes up the sheer detective-story slack. Sooner or later, readers (some of them, or most of them) will suspect the presence of a "mastermind," a person in the background who is the real directing force. Wolfert is the plant for that person. If Wolfert is not there, the reader seeking, or even feeling, the presence behind the scenes of a directing force would turn to Diedrich. Diedrich should not be suspected *merely because he is the only one available to suspect*. Someone else should be available to *absorb* this suspicion. Someone else should be in the story to do the dirty work—as I said, to take up the slack in the reader's conscious *or unconscious* groping for the truth. [. . .]

Of course, you might say that Wolfert could be eliminated and the old lady given the double psychological function—of preparing for the full acceptance of the *theme* and of giving the reader someone to blame for all the detective-story *illusions and tricks*. But this, in my opinion, would be bad. It would overload the old lady, and it would gravely dilute her more important function. It is better to have two people, each serving an entirely different psychological purpose.

Perhaps it will be clearer if I say it this way: you know what a fuse is in a fuse-box. It's the thing that warns of danger, and by blowing prevents trouble. In a way, Wolfert is the detective-story fuse—the safety-valve *in the reader's mind*, to take on the overload. Whenever the reader gets too close to the truth, Wolfert may relieve the strain.

Don't think I feel Diedrich is immune from suspicion, with or without Wolfert to distract the reader. As you know, it has been many, many years since I have put much stock in a so-called "surprise criminal." If a story, naturally and without straining, provides a surprise criminal, well and good; but a surprise criminal per se is outmoded—it is part of the more artificial trickery in a detective story that, in my opinion, we have outgrown. Yet, I think you will be surprised to learn eventually how many people do not even think of Diedrich as the directing force. He has a good cloak of psychological innocence, and

Wolfert helps in this respect. And even those readers who do not fall for Wolfert and who unerringly spot Diedrich's true place in the story—even those readers will never be *sure*. That very uncertainty, on top of their suspicion, will add immeasurably to the suspense. [. . .]

I am anxious about your final assessment of Wolfert's function. Please let me know how you feel about it after reading the above. Remember that to accomplish his part in the story, as I see it, Wolfert does not have to be present all the time. If you go back through the outline, I think you will discover that Wolfert is present *more than you thought*—another proof of his camouflage qualities, of his taking up the slack. To belabor a point, purely in the interests of getting over to you what I mean, think of Wolfert this way: what is the most successful type of advertising layout? That type of layout which you do not *see*. The layout, the abstract layout, which exerts its influence but which does not *obtrude* as a layout. Wolfert is the same way. His seeming unimportance is his real importance.

Now, to Howard, and again I shall try to make words express the intangibles of feeling: Howard is *not* an enigma—not in the sense that Jim Haight, for example, was and had to be an enigma. Jim Haight *had* to be an obscure character: his motives could not be revealed. But Howard's motives stand out crystal clear. Howard is, as you say, a pretty decent sort. He should have the reader's sympathy, and that sympathy should never be broken or destroyed. But for all Howard's decency, as you put it, there is a chink in his armor. He has these blackouts, which have produced a phobia in him and a guilt complex. He is under great mental pressure, and this gives him from time to time a feeling of unbalance. This 95 percent sanity and 5 percent potential insanity is very important. When it looks as if Howard is really behind all the crimes, there must be a possible acceptance on the part of the reader that Howard *could* be insane— in fact, Ellery actually says he is. Ellery therefore has to believe it is possible.

Yet, the over-all feeling about Howard is that he's a good guy—but a good guy with great troubles, a good guy who is forced constantly to fight those troubles and who may, or *may not*, be licking them. I agree with you that Howard, up to and including his committing suicide, should retain the reader's sympathy. How then explain his, what you call, unreasonable, selfish, really stupid attitude to Ellery in the blow-up scene?

The explanation is this—it was clear to me and I thought it was clear by implication in the outline: obviously, Howard knows he lied, knows he let Ellery down. That very knowledge, based on Howard's being decent, is what caused him to go into an insane tantrum, to upbraid Ellery violently. What does a really good guy do when he is forced, or thinks he is forced, to do a despicable act? He loses his maturity temporarily and reverts to being emotionally a child; he sets up a defense mechanism. And what form does this defense mechanism take? The person who *knows he is wrong* promptly accuses someone else of the guilt.

He takes out his own guilt on an innocent person. God, Man, this happens all the time: it is the most common form of *adjusting* a guilt complex.

It is analogous to something you yourself wrote in your own letter. Let me quote verbatim your own words: "You have a curtly Olympian way of saying I never told you something that always makes me feel slinky-guilty instantly, *and I begin covering up like mad before I think it out.*" There's your explanation for Howard's action—the cases are not the same, *but the principle of reaction is.* Howard's action *might be*, as you say, the hallmark of an unbalanced mind; that possibility is good, even essential, to the story; but Howard's action might also be—in fact, is—the hallmark of a perfectly normal human person who fights back, in an extremity, by blaming someone else, taking it out on someone else, just because he knows damn well he's not only wrong but worse (and this just exerts pressure on him) that he's 100 percent wrong. Of course, Howard was sorry as hell after he had cooled down, but by that time Ellery was gone, and by the time Ellery came back, Sally had been murdered and Howard found himself so deep in his own self-torment and misery that the injustice he did Ellery no longer mattered; in the light of his having killed the woman he loved, the tantrum he directed at Ellery seems very trivial. [. . .]

I hope I've covered all your queries on the novel. If there are more, or if I have omitted any, keep firing away. It goes without saying that you must get from me all I can possibly give you in the way of understanding the events, motivations, etc. (And you wanted me to send you a *short* outline!)

A little more that has just occurred to me on Howard: unlike Jim Haight, Howard's motives are not concealed. Everything he does stems from his two great problems: one, his blackouts and the mental torment they cause him; and two, his impossible and repressed love for Sally. These two crosses which he bears causes him to act the way he does—a decent guy who is forced, or thinks he is forced, to do indecent things; a decent guy who will stop at nothing—who will steal, lie, anything, to protect Sally and keep their own code of honor.

Remember, too, the enormous problem of making it appear *at all times* as if Howard is equally capable of good and evil, equally capable of being a genuinely good guy and a person irrational enough to be guilty of the worst crimes in the world. This necessity of making Howard fit two absolutely diverse characters is achieved by his blackouts. Understand clearly that Howard himself must at all times think himself capable of the most reprehensible actions; Howard must believe in his Jekyll-and-Hyde personality, and the reader must accept that split personality, accepting both the good Howard and the evil Howard with equal conviction. Remember, too, that Howard can never seriously doubt his capacity for evil, even including murder, while he is under the influence of a blackout. That is the key to Howard's dual role, and it is also one of Diedrich's most effective weapons, since Diedrich can always *impose* a blackout on Howard and thereby make Howard himself believe he (Howard) is really guilty of the things he is accused of having done.

Again, now that I think of it, you could say that a blackout theme, or any version of amnesia, is old hat. But again the proof of the pudding lies in what is done with a seemingly hackneyed idea. Diedrich's *use* of Howard's susceptibility to amnesia attacks struck me as new and even startling—at least, to the best of my knowledge, I do not recall amnesia being handled the way it is in *Ten Days' Wonder*; nor do I think that amnesia has been treated as a basis of character development, integrated with plot purpose, as it has been in *Ten Days' Wonder*. Or, to put it another way, the whole story would not be possible without the amnesia springboard—proving that development of the story arises *inevitably* from, among other stimuli, the amnesia. One incident follows another, not as a mere series of incidents strung together, but because each succeeding incident is not possible without the preceding ones. [. . .]

ALL OUR BEST TO ALL OF YOU. The caps are intended to make up for my sheer inability to go on or to elaborate.

DAN

1948: Enter the Cat

April 1948. Dannay no longer has to defend his *Ten Days' Wonder* treatment; Lee has moved from questioning Dannay's choices to completing a draft of the novel. The next letter is Lee's extended defense of his manuscript and offers his justification for the choices he made in turning Dannay's scenario into a fully realized story. He sounds one of the eternal themes of his collaboration with Dannay: The need for a free hand when writing. The line separating Dannay's contribution from Lee's tended to get smudged, and tempers flew because of this. Dannay was pained by the liberties Lee took with his carefully worked out conceptions; Lee felt constricted by Dannay's choices and made changes to bring much-needed plausibility and reality to what he believed were unrealistic and unworkable situations and characters. Their goal in dividing the labor—a peaceful collaboration in which each could play to his strength—was never achieved. Defense and accusation were Dannay and Lee's two dominant responses to each other.

Once again, letters are missing, but it seems that Dannay took issue with the "father-image interpretation, the psychological approach" Lee used to illustrate Howard Van Horn's relationship with his father Diedrich. To this reader, Lee's use of psychology is dead-on, and provides a realistic base for the theological daring of Dannay's ideas. Together they created an Ellery who possesses a level of psychological realism far beyond that of his fictional peers, and paved the way for the troubled, self-doubting detectives of today.

Stephen Dannay is a newborn. All is well in the Dannay household for the moment. Stephen's problems, stemming from severe brain damage at birth, will become sadly apparent in the months and years that follow.

Friday April 16 [1948]

Dear Dan:

[. . .] You say "The hall was an odorous memorial to departed feet" is "out of key," "ineffective," and "tends to spoil the very good stuff that surrounds it." I've reread the line in context and I don't agree. I could take the line out to please you, certainly; but this very minor, unimportant example—by admission on both our parts—raises a major, important question: Is pleasing you, in the face of my strong affirmative opinion that the line is in key, effective, and helps the stuff that surrounds it, to be my rule-of-thumb? We divided ourselves into rigid-boundaried "zones" just because our differences of opinion on basic matters of both plot and writing were so strong that we found it impossible to reconcile them either in principle or in practice. In the face of this, pleasing each other is pointless. We can only do, in our respective provinces, what pleases ourselves. [. . .]

My character conception of the old man pushing the mop: I think we would both agree that this point is most unimportant by itself, but it happens that your specific criticism raises a derivative point which goes to the heart of one of my big problems in doing this story. You say: "The characterization could have been one which awakened and developed a sympathy in the reader—a sympathy for humans in general and by transference *a sympathy for Howard in particular.*" You'll remember that I raised the question of Howard's character and its potentialities for raising sympathy in the reader long before I sat down to the typewriter. We had some correspondence about it which left me uneasy, and the uneasiness grew to major proportions the more I studied the outline. I soon recognized what it was that was bothering me. I saw that I was bothered not merely by Howard's denial of Ellery but *by everything you had Howard doing.* It wasn't that he fell in love with Sally; he laid her. Of course you had to have him lay her; your detective-story line demanded it. But a man who lays his father's wife can't possibly be construed as an admirable character. Fell in love with her? Yes; that would be beyond his control. But going to bed with her was not beyond his control. Anything wrong with this plotwise? No. *But it paints a certain type of character: a weakling.* Even this might have been sublimated away if what you called on Howard to do thereafter was not weak, but strong.

But no; he didn't go to his father and tell him what he'd done, which a strong man would have done; he didn't *go away*, which a strong man might also have done. [. . .] So you invent the background story designed to give him a positive and compelling reason for not telling his father: he doesn't want to hurt the old man, he owes him too much, etc. None of this, of course, precludes his just getting the hell out of the house; but you couldn't have him get out, so his love for Sally was designed to hold him there. Now I submit that none of this is *wrong*—far from it; it's great. *Only it doesn't give you the character you apparently wanted: a sympathetic one.* For one thing, a man who lays his father's wife but then can't tell the father because he doesn't want to hurt him and owes him too much can hardly arouse our *sympathy*, certainly not our sympathy in the sense of the reader's rooting for the character. If it arouses our sympathy at all, it can only be *a feeling sorry for his screwed-up weaknesses.* The one who really arouses our sympathy is the father. Howard becomes a sort of Hamlet—only a sort; but he is sufficiently like Hamlet in his indecisiveness to point an interesting parallel. But he is definitely unlike Hamlet in that he *never* resolves his indecisiveness. You'll say I'm being unfair, that he does resolve it at least in his action of faking another robbery to cover up the loss of the necklace, presumably again *to keep Diedrich from learning the truth.* If you conceived of Howard at all as a "strong" character, it could only be in this sense—his almost hysterical desire to keep his father from learning the truth. But whether that represented strength to you or not, I can only say that that *reason* points to a weakling. Weaklings are capable of great strengths sometimes, oddly enough in order to hold on to their weaknesses. [. . .]

How do you get sympathy for a weakling? The more I thought about it, the less I saw the answer . . . that is, an answer that didn't involve a pretty drastic approach. To me, the answer grew clear: the only possibility of getting sympathy for him was to make him the creature of forces beyond his control. A man who is weak "of his free will" can't possibly be "sympathetic"; a man who is weak because he is the product of his environment might be. What constituted Howard's "environment"? Obviously, Diedrich; that was in the story to begin with. So I suggested that Howard had been dominated from childhood by his father. I suggested that Howard had a "father-complex" and so on—all tending to put the blame for Howard's weakness not on Howard but on Diedrich. I hoped in this way to get sympathy for Howard even when he was doing damned unsympathetic things. I can't say I was too successful, yes. But at least it was an attempt to get a reasonable, authentic, recognizable basis for Howard's doing what you had to have him do, toward the end of making him seem not a cowardly, sniveling weakling but a confused, manipulated poor human who might have been strong and admirable if he's been raised by a man who didn't insist on dominating those he loved . . . It was this whole train of thought, incidentally, which led to the "father-image" extension in the detective-story line. I have now gone out of the point I started with and into another of your points, but these things are integrated and I can't help it. [...]

To get back to the old man with the mop, who now seems very far away: Here, too, I was being consistent with my conception of Howard as the product of his environment. I had conjured up for Howard, for the reasons stated, an environment essentially *hostile*. The old man simply symbolized that hostility extended into the outer world. No one can tell me that the Howard you painted in your outline is in tune with world around him. He just isn't. He's at odds with it at every point, or he wouldn't act the way you had him act, or had to have him act. So he's at odds with the old derelict in the flophouse, too. That's also why I had Howard at odds with the environment he found himself in in Paris ten years before. It's why, when he got back and the war started, he was at odds with his own home town. And I didn't have to "strain." The material was there in the outline. The only thing is, you didn't—from my viewpoint, of course—realize your material. Well, perhaps in your province realizing material character-wise isn't necessary or even desirable. But surely it is in mine. In fact, it must be in mine. Not to think out a character in terms of his whole life as well as in terms of the specific acts your plot calls upon him to commit is simply not doing a writing job. But, you may say, it brings up other material I know nothing about, didn't plan on, and so on—material that even, as you charge, causes "serious disjointments of the original situation." [...]

Howard's killing himself triply: You ask why, and say it may even strike some readers "as slightly ludicrous." You say "simple hanging" does the trick, "and in my opinion more sharply and more tragically than with embroidery." I disagree on all counts, very strongly indeed. I don't mean that "simple hanging" wouldn't have done the trick, in the sense that it would have accomplished Howard's suicide. I do mean that I can't find a single aspect of that passage which could strike anyone as ludicrous to any degree; that simple hanging would not have done the trick "more sharply and more tragically," quite the reverse; and that, far from the wrist-slashing and the shooting-through-the-mouth being "embroidery" (a word in this context I think you'll understand my finding not very kind), they are virtually mandatory in the psychological picture I have painted of Howard. The suicide for psychoneurotic reasons, once he makes up his mind, is tenaciously set on death. His anxiety to die takes the form very frequently of multiple methods. The spectacle of such a suicide slashing his wrists, hanging himself, and shooting himself all at about the same time is a commonplace of psychoneurotic literature. I even exercised restraint. Often they'll take poison, too! And, as I had somebody say, "He sure wanted to die in the worst way." It's quite true. To escape from his problems is the great compulsion, and he makes damned sure he escapes. Ludicrous? I'd say sympathy!

Now I have to get into pretty much all the rest of your points together, as they all tie in with one another. But before I do I want to cover the ground raised by your charge that I didn't discuss the psychological interpretation I imposed on the story, that I committed myself to it without even giving you a chance to participate in the decision, etc. The charge, of course, taken at its bald face-value, is true. But the whole picture, as against the surface, while I don't expect to satisfy your wishes or opinions, should clear the fog away for you.

The idea did not spring full-grown, at a given moment. It grew as I fumbled my way through what I conceived as the lacks and inconsistencies of the original outline and even as I was writing. I can't say exactly when it emerged in its full stature as an idea. I do remember that I did a lot of rewriting and fixing up as I went along. [. . .] When that period was over, the work was so far advanced that the problem of discussion took on an entirely different aspect. I was, as you say, committed to it; you can hardly live with a thing day in and day out for months as I did, without becoming committed to something you believe is inevitable, right, and desirable. To have broached the whole thing to you then, in all its ramifications, was frankly beyond me. For one thing, it couldn't be broached adequately in letters and the phone would take many hours. Do you remember, not the hours, but the days you and I spent on controversial points a lot more trivial than this one? [. . .] It would have been all but impossible even to explain myself to you separated by 3000 miles; it actually called for long discussions and references to the written material itself. And there was always the pressure of being behind the due date, not to mention my own continuous weariness from sheer overwork.

And at the end, as I said—what? We would have got into an argument, probably bitter (did I say "probably"?) over our respective [. . .] provinces and then we would have been—as always—hung up. What to do? Whose way to take? Whose right to dictate? Where do you stop and I begin? And I would have to say: To take out the father-image interpretation, the psychological approach, would be impossible for me. It's the only way I could write the story; it's the only approach that makes what I must work with possible to work with. You might say: "But it's a mistake to elaborate Ellery into a psychiatric detective or even an intellectual detective with psychiatric facets!" (as you did). I would say you must share as much responsibility for that mistake as I do [. . .] Of course this must be frustrating to you, and believe me when I say in all and unreserved earnestness that I understand that frustration. But, Dan, if the way we work and the fundamental differences between our viewpoints on important questions have their very real potentialities for frustrating you, they also do the same for me. In one important sense they potentially frustrate me a hell of a lot more than they do you. Because in the way we work you have one tremendous advantage over me. When you start your work, and while you're doing your part of the work, *you are a completely free agent*. You are free to do exactly what you please, for the choice of your material you have the world to choose from, only yourself to please, and no one to account to for your choices. [. . .] You have accused me often of presenting you with accomplished facts; I say to you that every time you do a novel outline you are presenting me with an accomplished fact that puts mine into the shade. You don't merely give me a basic idea. You don't merely give me a set of characters. You give me a basic idea worked out to the last detail, with a set of characters so completely delineated that you even indicate their type of dialogue. You give me alpha through omega. You give me, really, not an outline but a blueprint. [. . .]

In the case of *Ten Days' Wonder*, on the day you handed me the outline, *I didn't even know what your basic idea was*. You had discussed the Ten Commandments idea with me many months before; you didn't ask my opinion, you just told me about it. I expressed my opinion just the same; I said I liked the idea. Then a long time went by. Other ideas were mentioned. [. . .] When you told me you were working on the outline you didn't tell me a thing about it. You mentioned it vaguely and I refrained from asking you since to have asked you to go into the thing would have raised all the ghosts we tried to lay when we decided to separate our spheres rigorously. And so, on the appointed day, I got the thing: fresh, complete, to the last period—to the chapter headings! [. . .] Did you find it necessary to discuss with me, for instance, the advisability of characterizing this as Ellery's last case? Surely this transcends your province? The question of Ellery's last case is a question of policy, and in policy I am as equally concerned as you. I still think it's a mistake. I let it go at the time, I brought it up once, later, you indicated that it was the logical development of the story and Ellery's fix, I let it go again. And I did it your way, even though I thought and still think it's unwise, unnecessarily quixotic, and raises possible complications for the future. [. . .]

It's been that way ever since the early days when you started doing complete outlines. I have to work with characters I don't believe in, doing things I may not think they'd do in some instances, or for reasons that strike me as superficial or wrong. Not all, of course, or even most; but the problem is always there, in greater or lesser degree. I must accept solutions I violently disagree with. There is, for example, a hole in the solution of *Ten Days' Wonder* which I didn't find until I was writing the solution itself. It's a hole most people won't see. To have fixed it would undoubtedly have meant the addition of a great deal of material, the change of a lot that already existed. Frankly, I said the hell with it and I covered it up. This is the wrong attitude; I loathe it in myself. But with the way we work, with what stands between us and has stood between us for twenty years, and with the pressures, and every other damned factor that existed, I just didn't have the energy or the desire to raise the question. Wrong, wrong. But I submit that it's a result of *us*—of what we've been to and against each other—rather than a result of me exclusively, or you exclusively. [. . .]

In this book I had a particularly tough time—from this standpoint—not only with Howard but with Sally. I don't know whether it will come to you as a surprise, but are you aware that in all the business of Howard's "denying" Ellery and putting him deliberately in jeopardy of a charge of grand larceny, you simply neglected in your outline to say a damned word about Sally's part in it? Wasn't she equally responsible with Howard for that lie? Why didn't she speak up? Why was she silent? All right, you'll say that it was because she, too, like Howard, had the overpowering compulsion not to "hurt" Diedrich by letting the story of the adultery come out. (For my money that makes her out as big a stinker as Howard—even bigger, because at least he had the "guts" to lie outright; she was so cowardly she didn't say anything at all.) But even granting all that, you didn't even mention Sally in the outline in this connection—even though it was her necklace, she had given it to Howard, she had been present when Howard urged Ellery to pawn it, she had urged him to pawn it herself. The reason you didn't mention it, I take it, is that at the time the lie became necessary, plot-wise, it was "cleaner" to put it all on Howard, since it was Howard's lie that gave him the appearance of having borne false witness, etc., and for Sally's part in it to have been brought up at that point must have seemed to you to muddy and weaken the point as it applied to Howard. So you left it out.

But I couldn't. I *had* to say something about Sally in the book itself. To have said nothing would have been—I hardly know how to characterize it—a shockingly glaring omission, from any standpoint. All you were concerned with was the plot. I had to be concerned, whether I wanted to or not, with the people, Ellery, the whole scene and situation. [. . .]

Dan, you tell me that "one of the keys to the reader's heart—the master key, in this book—is the completely unalloyed love of Howard and Sally for each other." It's on this point that we split—right down the middle. I say that you can't have your cake and eat it, too. If this was a completely "unalloyed" love—by which I suppose you mean pure, deep, without slag or evil—then Howard and Sally should have been unalloyed characters by extension. If their love was so goddamned big, and pure, and deep, where did your outline bring it out? What action proved your point? What series of actions? That they fell in love and slept with each other over a romantic weekend? I don't think that would convince anybody, considering the circumstances. It was a guilty love—that was your whole point. To have raised it from the slough of "guilty love" into "completely unalloyed" love Howard and Sally would have had to do exactly what you didn't want them to do, which was to tell all to Diedrich, the man they wronged (and he was wronged even if he was the Devil himself), face the music, and try to solve their problem in a decent way. That would have taken the curse off their guilt. Or maybe your point is that, true, it was a guilty love, but a guilty love can be "unalloyed," "genuine and full," too. Let's grant that. But can you get sympathy for a guilty love that hides? That persists in hiding? That will steal and frame and put a man in jeopardy of his freedom in order to keep hiding? You say that "circumstances can be more powerful than love"? I say again, you can't have your cake and eat it, too. Sure circumstances can. But then what happens to the love? It couldn't rise above circumstances. It can be "crushed," as you say, by such forces "as conscience, morals, human frailty." If it can be crushed by conscience, then it wasn't a very worthy love to begin with. By morals? Then it was immoral. By human frailty? Then it was frail. It was anything, in other words, than the "kind of love that would make them wholly sympathetic characters," that would make "the reader have something to pull for." It was anything but admirable. Human? Oh, yes! But not everything "human" is admirable or arouses sympathy. These people were weak, Dan, and I could only write them from that jumping-off place.

Sally was tough for me. I had to supply the streak of what I called "ruthlessness" in order to justify her silence, when Ellery was put in jeopardy. I had to make her protest several times that her only concern after the event was Diedrich. *I had to make Ellery see her—and Howard—as I saw them; otherwise I couldn't have written this book at all.* [. . .]

You talk about "pure tragedy," and also about "the forces which actually exist in life." The two aren't necessarily synonymous. If he loved her truly, you say, in essence, that would make for pure tragedy. Since I changed it to the fact that he didn't truly love her but only *thought* he did, when all the time his motivation went deep into a lifelong psychological problem, you say the tragedy is no longer pure but "confusing." I don't really know what you mean by "pure" tragedy; I do know that a man's doing what Howard did on the basis of a *false unconscious* reason is tragedy as it exists in real life, because that's what most of us do. [. . .] I think the whole "father-image" conception with all its implications and ramifications—as I said—"enriches" the book to a marked degree, both as character material and for its meaning in the solution.

Let me put it this way: you feel that "all this" came about "because" I "felt that Howard must have a father-image motivation." [. . .] I chose the father-image, or rather the father-image chose me, because it followed naturally and almost inevitably from what was there. Of course, if I hadn't known about such things as father-images I couldn't have chosen it nor could it have chosen me. But then I think—and I know you will completely disagree with me—the resulting book would have been inferior to its present version. And when I say inferior I mean not only as a book about people but also as a mystery.

That's sticking my neck out about as far as it can go. [. . .]

I agree that the tenth chapter is too long, but merely to say "cut it" doesn't do the job. What would you cut? It was necessary to go into the long long scene between Diedrich and Ellery in exhaustive detail or leave out things which needed explaining. I followed your outline in this very faithfully. The only additions I made concerned the father-image. These don't take up much space. I doubt if much could be cut out of the tenth chapter; and if the cuts were trifling (and if major cuts were made in the preceding nine chapters) you'd have a book even more overbalanced than it is now!

Let it go, Dan, let it go. You and I have had plenty of troubles in this kind of business. Let's not drag it out. [. . .]

We are just delighted with your news about the baby. He must be coming along awfully fast and I should think you and Bill would be in seventh heaven. It's fantastically soon for him to be coming home from hospital, considering his start. He sounds like a strong, determined youngster, and Kaye and I have been rooting for him like anything since you phoned that night. [. . .]

Brother, I'm THROUGH FOR THE DAY.

MANNY

The Adventures of Ellery Queen left the airwaves in May 1948. In the course of its erratic nine-year run, the peripatetic program had jumped from CBS to NBC, returned to CBS, and then spent a final season on ABC before expiring.

Sandy Stronach, mentioned in the following letter from Dannay, worked in the radio department of the ad agency Young & Rubicam before moving to the William Morris Agency in 1947. Despite his efforts, EQ never returned to the airwaves.

The show's unique "Challenge to the Listener" format—in which EQ would stop the show and ask the celebrity guests of the week if they could solve the mystery—was later adapted for the 1975-76 television series.

Dannay's recounting of his conversation with Stronach regarding the EQ radio show and its competition provides a fascinating look at the radio business just as it began its decline. It also offers a vivid picture of Dannay's relentless theorizing about the EQ character and how best to make the detective reflect the times.

The outline mentioned is for *Cat of Many Tails*. Dannay's original title for the novel was *Off With His Head!*—a reference to his beloved Lewis Carroll. The "December short story" is "The Dauphin's Doll," published in the December 1948 issue of *EQMM*.

June 24, 1948

Dear Man:

[. . .] Stronach finally got the story out of ABC—why they dropped Queen. It seems that ABC have been pressed for some time economically and had to drop some shows. The question was which. So they conducted a sort of survey or inquiry, or whatever you want to call it, on mystery shows to determine which should be kept on the air and which should be dropped.

Their survey revealed that the only popular mystery shows—the ones the listeners kept coming back to—have two essential characteristics: (1) there must be a central detective character; and (2) that character must be alive, must have the human-being qualities that make listeners feel that they are participating in the adventures of a real person, one they know and like, and one they want to hear about, watch, etc.

Now get this: ABC believes in the results of their survey—there is no use arguing with them or, for the moment, even questioning their findings. As Stronach said, they can document their findings, so far as radio is concerned, and we can't.

ABC first dropped *The Clock*—because it had no central character. Then they dropped us. We had a central character, but here the disappointment to ABC was even keener. Our central character, ABC concluded, was not a real living person in the sense that other central detective characters on radio are. Ellery is quiet, intellectual, without eccentricities that appeal to listeners—well, you know what they mean.

Naturally, I asked what human qualities they found in other radio shows. Well, take *The Fat Man*: ABC admits that Smart, who acts the part, is no great shakes as an actor, that the stories are no great shakes—but the Fat Man, they say, is the kind of person the listeners have taken to their hearts. He has eccentricities: a peculiar but apparently likable laugh; peculiar mannerisms; etc. *The Thin Man* also has *human* qualities—Stronach reeled them off, but for the life of me I can't seem to remember them now; of course, Nora helps, the sex helps, and so on.

Take *Mr. and Mrs. North*: the listeners *love* Mrs. North. She's a detective-story Mrs. Ace, malapropish, screwball, flighty—and so on. She's always getting her husband into hot water, always finding corpses in the most unlikely places, and always she is *gay*. Again, you know what I mean; I'm trying to put down my conversation with Stronach, as filtered, so to speak, through ABC.

Take [*Mister District Attorney*]: now there's a character! He dominates everything and everybody around him; he's strong, aggressive—why do you know, Man, everybody calls him sir!

Then take Ellery: by comparison, he's weak, colorless, deliberately understated, and so on and so on.

Now let's get serious: there is no point in questioning whether or not ABC is right, half-right, or wrong. We know that radio is a sheeplike industry, completely formularized, and so on. Had the Queen show on ABC happened to hit an impressive—a really impressive—rating, then suddenly the very qualities ABC found bad would have been the qualities that "made" the show; or they would have said Queen is the exception to the rule—successful despite its faults.

But we both know that however exaggeratedly or even falsely ABC has analyzed the situation, there is a serious and fundamental truth in their argument. [. . .]

Stronach has an explanation for Queen's radio success for years despite Ellery's colorless and lifeless personality. He thinks we were successful because we brought to radio a unique format, but that after all these years, the format has simply worn out. As he says, by this time all the millions of listeners are so familiar with the Queen format, take it so much for granted now, that it no longer has any element of freshness—indeed, just the opposite, it is now hackneyed. And what they want now, what they listen to week after week, is character. Stronach also mentioned that ABC feel that is the reason for the complete slump in the *Suspense* show; while *Suspense* stuck to big time weekly guest stars, they got by; when they gave up big name principals, they became a show without a central character—so, boom.

I agree that our unique-for-radio format was a factor, an important one. But [. . .] I think there was—and I'll try to put it as clearly as I can, using bromide-words— sincerity, integrity, purity in the earlier Queen shows that the last couple of years of Queen shows did not have—at least, in the sense I mean. This purity of technique got over with the listeners, and Ellery as a character fitted in with this purity of technique. Am I making myself at all clear?

The Queen shows of the last couple of years had—to my mind—a certain phoniness and a certain hybrid quality. I always found it phony to hear the Queen show start with a high-sounding opening about good citizenship, the fight against bigotry, and so [on], with Ellery a defender of the faith and a public-spirited crime-buster, and then seldom hear this theme actually borne out by the plots. [. . .] The truth is—again, my opinion, you understand—we did not have to counteract the pressure against bloody shows; we never were that type of show. Our distinction was—and let me say again that I am trying to get over a point the best I can off the cuff—our distinction was that we offered a higher-level mystery show, a pure detective show, and our central character fitted that conception. [. . .]

You have known my feelings in this regard for long time, but you never agreed; and since you were running the show, and I had agreed not to interfere, I could do no more than weakly voice my opinion on those rare occasions when you gave me an opportunity. You always spoke of "radio values"; I always spoke of the true merchandise we had to sell—the qualities that, for better or worse, are Queen and not imitative or compromise. [. . .]

Now, this whole question of character—which, as you understand, is not a new question at all—has its most important bearing for the actual moment on Queen novels. I expect to send you a 75-page outline very soon now, and this is as good a time as any for me to make a confession to you.

I have made a compromise [. . .] and I am sensitively aware of the danger of compromise. I could not do an out-and-out detective story without any Queen feeling whatever—that, I think, would have been wrong. On the other hand, I did try to cut a path between a Queen novel and a straight magazine-movie detective story. Whether I succeeded or not, I no longer know. I have reached that stage in the work where, as always happens, my perspective is completely gone and all I want to do is finish.

How does this tie in with the present question of Ellery's character? Naturally, Man, I could not tamper with Ellery's character without first consulting you in all its possible aspects. Ellery remains Ellery in the new novel—not a new kind of Ellery; but he is under an unusual emotional stress (not love) and this gives him a definitely human role to play. You will be able to tell better when you have read the outline.

But the big point is this: that it would be wise indeed for both of us to take stock most carefully and most thoroughly at this time. We both have the feeling that a lifetime's work, in all fields, is sort of crumbling around us. [. . .]

We have something of our own—the years have proved that. We must develop that which is Queen—yes, with changes. With perhaps a new approach, but we can't suddenly transform Ellery into the Fat Man, or the Thin Man, or Mr. D.A., or Perry Mason. We've got to maintain the *basic purity* of Ellery— with those modifications which 1948 demands. [. . .]

By the way: how about the December short story? And bear in mind, Man, that even after you get started on the new novel, you *must* arrange your schedule to slice in the shorts—otherwise, another year will go by before we can have the advantage of magazine publication.

All our best. Steve will be circumcised July 3rd—the earliest date we could get an operating room in a New York hospital! No one but the doctors (2) and the rabbi will be permitted in the room, and we will take Steve home the same day. He went on regular cow's milk today!

DAN

June 30, 1948

Dear Dan:

[. . .] The shows I was responsible for *were* different from those done when you were doing the plots. The difference lay in two factors:

(1) The radio values you put between quotation marks; and

(2) A humanized Ellery.

The plots you worked out for the earlier Queen shows were largely mathematical puzzles, in which the "factors" of the puzzle were expressed in terms of people. The emphasis was placed on problem and cerebration. There were long scenes of explanatory or expository dialogue, essential to the kind of puzzle you were doing. *Things* didn't happen; *ideas* happened. In most cases, when the idea-happening necessarily had to express itself in terms of things-happening, the things-happening were not shown but were merely talked about after the events. [. . .]

I went out after [. . .] stories of people—unusual or unusually interesting characters, and/or conflicting human relationships, and/or recognizable and interesting backgrounds—a synthesis of persons, relations, and events rather than a puzzle-in-logic. I retained the formula and the format; the difference was that where your stories were virtually *all* formula and format, the ones I produced reduced their importance in the sense that the other values were enlarged—so that the total effect was to get a better balance of elements, radio-wise.

Now you say that this was not good. I say I had a radio show to keep on the air, and that was the way to do it. I say that had I continued your type of show, or had we continued your type of show together, we would have been off the air long ago. [. . .] But if what radio success today demands is a flashy or sensational character, then either Ellery has to be changed radically into something completely different from the original concept—a job I have never felt it was my place or responsibility to do alone—or we have to create a new character altogether without the "stigma" of the "Ellery" handle. [. . .]

You say "The truth is we did not have to counteract the pressure against bloody shows; we never were that type of show." Oh, didn't we? That has been my beef all along; that we never were that type of show but that we were being punished as if we had been. [. . .] The essence of my complaint has been for two years now that the drive against mysteries in radio has been completely unselective, punishing the innocent along with the guilty; and the only ones who have escaped—especially among the guilty—are those like [*Mister District Attorney*] whose *success*—in the typical American way—puts it beyond the reach of proselytizing groups. What do you mean we didn't have to counteract the pressure? The question wasn't were we guilty; the question was, were we being pressed? We were. So I had to do something to counteract the pressure. [. . .]

The whole tone of your letter, as it relates to the radio question, is that I have failed. You seem to take a rather regretful view of it, but the feeling is that you always knew it would and of course, it did. "I told you so" sticks out all over the letter . . . well-hedged with "in my opinions," of course, and "to my minds," but that is a device of long standing with you.

Well, I haven't failed, Dan. I kept this show on the air for over 4 years with no help from you. For all but 27 shows of the some 200 that aired under my eye, we were sponsored—yes, and I did it under adverse conditions in lousy time-spots with nickel-nursers. At the first sign of trouble you let me have it. And you are ready to take almost anything to get the show back on the air. Well, I'm not. I think Stronach and the Morris office have sold you a bill of goods; or rather you've sold yourself one. The fact is, Morris has lifted hardly a finger to do anything really good in the way of selling this show for many years; when the pinch came last fall the best Murray could come up with was a sustainer deal— and last fall there were shows being sold commercially right and left; and now, when the market is really bad, we get the "it's the show's fault" routine. Funny, it never was before. [. . .]

I received your novel outline, and I have given it a first reading. Simultaneously, the galleys on *Ten Days' Wonder* came in from Little, Brown and I want to get them off before tackling the new novel's problems.

I will write to you in detail my reactions at a later date, but meanwhile there is one point which stood out for me as an immediate problem which I must call to your attention.

An extremely important point in your plot revolves about a physician's having delivered his own three babies.

I have been under the impression for many years that no physician is allowed to deliver his own children. It is either a matter of professional ethics or downright against the law, or both—I'm not sure. Did you do any research on this? You made no attempt to give odd circumstances in explanation, which leads me to believe you assumed it was perfectly all right. I do know of a case or two in which a doctor has delivered a child of his wife's, but in each of these cases there was an extremely peculiar circumstance, an emergency, to explain it. One doctor I know of delivered his own child in the elevator of the hospital as he was taking his wife up to the check-in room—the baby came too fast and the wife couldn't hold it back. He had engaged another doctor to do the delivery and the doctor got there too late. In other words, in the emergency he couldn't help himself.

It is conceivable, then, that the doctor in your outline might have delivered one child under some similar circumstance, but three or even two would be a tremendous stretch.

If you were unaware of this, or did not consider it, would you check up on it in the next few days? Or, if you have some other explanation, or facts at variance with what I've written here, let me know what they are.

* * *

This has been a very bad time for me. The past fall and winter have left me pretty well exhausted, not only physically but in more important ways. On my return from San Francisco, I found it impossible to concentrate. I have spent most of the time doing chores around the house which I had had to neglect since moving in here, and trying to work things out for myself in my mind.

I've done a considerable amount of "working things out." I'll be 44 on my next birthday and this is no time in a man's life to kid himself—about anything. I think I've done a lot of growing up in the last few months, and high time, too. One thing I've learned is to stand on my own two feet. It's a lesson I needed, badly.

I will have the Christmas yarn for you well in advance of your deadline, which as I recall it was August 1. I am well aware of the necessity of slicing the missing shorts into my other work. I have not yet set my own schedule, as even a preliminary reading of your outline told me that I was going to have to do considerable research, on the psychiatrist background.

Bravo to Steve. He's really made it. Hope everything goes all right at the circumcision. No reason why it shouldn't. [. . .]

MANNY

July 2, 1948

Dear Man:

Your special deliver letter of June 30th arrived just as I was sitting down to dinner tonight. I glanced through it, but that was enough: my dinner was completely ruined; my stomach turned over.

Perhaps I ought to attempt no reply for at least a full day, but the hell with it. I simply am not going to stew about it for twenty-four hours, bring on even more colonic distress than I have now, and then write—or try to write—a reasoning, analytical letter. [. . .]

Your present appraisal of the old Queen shows is brutally unfair. Yes, a lot of them were puzzles—but not all of them. In fact, not nearly as many as you now think. And even the most cerebral of the puzzles were not merely mechanical plots. You'll find a hell of a lot more human interest in the old shows than you realize. Has it occurred to you that the farther away you get from the old shows in time, the more you are inclined to misjudge them?

Manny, I don't honestly think you have the slightest understanding of what I mean by "purity of technique." Purity of detective-story technique permits a certain type of phoniness—the type that excites wonder, produces color, baffles, perplexes, and so on. But this is not the kind of phoniness I find in radio shows that pretend to be realistic. Oh, what the hell. We could discuss this for a solid century, and still get nowhere. In quite a few of your letters to me, since you moved to Hollywood, you have pointed out how much you have grown up, how much you have learned. In this last letter of yours you say: "One thing I've learned is to stand on my own feet."

This sounds like a threat. Is that what it's meant to be? If so, what the hell do you have in mind? Why not come right out with it?

In these same letters you have said more than once that the only way to treat people is to get tough—that any other policy is interpreted as weakness, appeasement. Manny, this is a terribly dangerous philosophy. Learning how to get tough is not necessarily the equivalent of growing up, of maturing. Oh, you've learned to be tough, all right. It seems that lots of people who live in

Hollywood learn to be tough. I can just see how easy it is to confuse toughness with realism. The tougher you are with others, the more of a realist you are—is that it? Is that what you mean by growing up, by standing on your own feet? If that is what you have in mind, Man, you're wrong—dangerously wrong. I can even see the possibility that you may have interpreted some of my recent actions as the result of your get-tough policy. I'd hate to learn that this is true.

I cannot tell you how low I feel right now—about everything connected with Queen. We seem farther apart in understanding than ever before, and the geographical separation—forcing us to resort to long, involved and perpetually misunderstood letters—emphasizes the futility and despair in my mind. I approach each new problem with waning confidence, with increasing fears, with devastating doubt. Here, for example, I have just finished a grueling job on the new novel. It was a job particularly beset with difficulties, with new decisions to make, with compromises to hurdle. You have read the outline and the only thing I get from you is the raising of a doubtful point. I can only assume, as of old, that you do not like the job fundamentally—with the inevitable result, also as of old, that you will tend to fight against the story.

Well, Man, if it is true that you do not like the new novel, and if you feel as strongly about it as you have in the past about other novels, then again—the hell with it. It's okay with me. In fact, if you should happen to dislike the new novel intensely, then send back the whole fucking outline to me, and that's that. All that will be lost is my time, my work, and my health.

Nevertheless, for the record, let me answer the point you brought up. There is no law which prohibits an obstetrician from delivering his own children. Nor is it a matter of professional ethics. The only reason doctors don't generally deliver their own children is purely one of anxiety. Most doctors realize that it is dangerous to treat members of their own family—dangerous only in the sense that they are emotionally involved, and therefore are not able to maintain a completely objective and detached professional attitude. However, aside from emergencies, doctors often deliver their own children. I know one obstetrician— considered the finest young obstetrician in New York—who delivered both his children.

It is true that a doctor who insists on delivering his own children is a definite type. He must have tremendous confidence in himself. He must think himself above personal anxiety. He would be an egocentric person, probably also somewhat of an exhibitionist.

This type is precisely the type often found among psychiatrists.

Add to the above the following powerful motivation: we know at the end that while Dr. Cazalis insisted on taking care of his own wife and delivering his own children—*presumably* because he was fanatically anxious that nothing would go wrong—Dr. Cazalis actually had a definite motive in delivering his own children. That motive was to kill them. [. . .]

At this stage of each novel I am always conscious of the extraordinary paradox which I am constantly expected to resolve. Many times in the past you have urged me to hand you short outlines—you have even said, the shorter the better. And I have always replied that I cannot tell enough in a short outline. So I finally wind up giving you 75 or 80 pages—far too long, according to you.

Then, at the end of the writing of the novel, we inevitably wrangle over differences in interpretation, and so on. At that time you always say that there are lapses, omissions, and so on in the outline, and these omission by me caused differences in interpretation. [. . .]

As I wrote you, I fell two months behind on the magazine editing—in order to finish the outline of the new novel by July 1st. I simply must get to work on the magazine, or find myself in shit creek. It will take me the rest of July to select 25 stories, write the editorial comment, edit, and prepare the stories for the printer. By that time I'll be a complete wreck, or damn close to it. Maybe, perversely, things will look brighter to me then—I'll be too worn out to see how futile things are. Right now I can look twenty years of work square in the face and ask myself: Do I know a Goddam thing about what I'm doing? You tell me.

DAN

As with *Ten Days' Wonder*, the letters concerning *Cat of Many Tails* allow us to witness the birth—often difficult—of a masterpiece.

The majority of *Cat* is set in post-World-War-II Manhattan during one oppressively hot summer. The city teeters on the edge of chaos as The Cat—a strangler with a penchant for pink and blue silk cords—claims one victim after another. Ellery, still reeling from the effects of the Van Horn case, is unable to act, afraid to cause more damage, more deaths. He is stirred into action only when the Cat reaches a deadly paw into Harlem and a race riot is feared. Ellery starts tracking the Cat in earnest.

He's joined by newspaperman Jimmy McKell and Celeste Martin, each of whom has lost a sister to the Cat. He finds another ready convert to the cause in Dr. Edward Cazalis, whose niece was also one of the Cat's victims. Cazalis is an obstetrician who turned to psychology after a nervous breakdown in middle age. He creates and implements a survey of participating psychologists to help identify mental patients who fit the Cat's psychological profile. But their efforts are to no avail. Ellery is stymied until a discrepancy involving the birth date of one of the victims provides him with the clue he needs to predict the strangler's next target and to identity the Cat as none other than Dr. Cazalis. Cazalis is caught in the act and arrested.

Months after the resolution of the case, Ellery is at the New York Public Library, researching psychological matters for a new mystery novel. He discovers that Cazalis was attending a psychiatric convention in Switzerland when the Cat's murder spree began. The facts of the case proved that one man was responsible for all of the murders; therefore Cazalis was not the Cat.

But if it wasn't Cazalis . . .

Ellery travels to Vienna, Austria to speak to Dr. Bela Seligmann, Cazalis's friend and mentor. Ellery has certain ideas about Cazalis and the Cat, but he lacks hard evidence. Seligmann graciously agrees to listen and, based on his knowledge of Cazalis, weigh in on Ellery's theories.

After sharing his ideas about Cazalis's psychological make-up—all of which Seligmann tacitly agrees with—Ellery draws his conclusion: *Mrs.* Cazalis is the Cat. Her stillborn children had been delivered by her husband. In a late-flowering madness she set out to kill all the children that Cazalis had successfully brought into the world. Cazalis found this out and covered it up. He took the blame for his wife and pretended to be the Cat. Seligmann concurs with Ellery's conclusion.

Ellery places a call to his father in New York; the trial must be stopped in the interests of justice. Inspector Queen tells him that Dr. Cazalis and his wife have committed suicide. She smuggled poison into his jail cell, and that ended matters for good and all. Once again, Ellery is too late, and justice is frustrated. And, as in the Van Horn case, Ellery succumbs to despair.

He is saved by Dr. Seligmann. In what are arguably the most moving passages in the Queen *oeuvre*, Seligmann absolves the troubled detective of the guilt he feels, and offers him a centuries-old lesson in humility and perspective: *"There is one God, and there is none other but He."*

By the end of *Cat of Many Tails*, Ellery has been humbled and restored to his proper self. It's an amazing journey, one that has taken him far from his origins as a Harvard dandy with pince-nez, walking stick and a vocabulary well stocked with Greek and Latin quotations to this incarnation: a character of real depth, an older and wiser man who knows the limits as well as the strength of intelligence.

July 3, 1948

Dear Man:

Steve was circumcised early this morning and seems to be doing well. I had a chance to talk for a minute or two with our New York pediatrician (different of course from the obstetrician) and I asked about a doctor delivering his own children.

The pediatrician confirmed that there is no law against it; nor is it a matter of professional ethics. It is purely a matter of character. The doctor who insists (in actuality, not pretense) on delivering his own children would be one who is fanatical that his wife run not the slightest conceivable risk and that he, and he alone, can best take care of her. This, of course, brings us back to an egocentric person.

The pediatrician, however, did say this: that he thinks it is more uncommon than other doctors have led me to believe. [. . .]

In this outline I did not treat Cazalis as an egocentric, exhibitionistic, screwy kind of person. That would have pointed too obviously to him as the possible maniac-killer. I think the reader should be led to believe slowly but surely, or in a false flash of intuition, that Cazalis in the insane killer—this is part of the double-bluff, part of the protective coloration around Mrs. Cazalis. Because I liked this approach better, because I considered it more subtle, I visualized Cazalis as a sound person, leaving it to the reader to begin slowly to suspect him—he is the "obvious" psychological suspect. That is why I brought out the delivery-of-his-own-babies point late; if when the point comes out some readers find it strange, the strangeness will be completely explained in the end when readers learn that Cazalis had a definite motive for doing the unusual thing of delivering his own children.

All of this is perfectly clear to me, but I wouldn't be the least surprised to hear that I am not making it clear to you. I find it more and more difficult to make certain ideas clear at this time: I'm tired out, terrifically depressed in spirit by your letters, to say nothing of having plenty of troubles of my own. I barely slept a wink last night—my old insomnia is plaguing me again; and Bill and I were up at six this morning to bring Steve to the hospital. What without sleep, and low morale, and waiting a solid hour in the hospital waiting-room for word from the doctors that everything is all right, and hearing the little guy cry in pain at home now, I can tell you that I'm not very Pollyannish about anything. [. . .]

I had intended to attach a letter of comment, but I didn't even have time for that. But I think it would be wise now if I did throw out some comments I had intended to make.

(1) The significance of the first chapter: to put one murder on scene, yet without giving away anything about the murderer; to build up the scope and series-effect of the coming murders; and most important, to suggest how the murderer makes contact with strangers, wins their confidence, and so on. Once the reader sees how the murderer accomplished one crime, the reader can easily imagine how the murderer did it in all the succeeding crimes. This is further enlightened when the reader sees how Cazalis manages (as the Cat would have) the tenth murder. I considered for a while putting the second murder on scene— say, in the middle of the book; but I decided against it. The present form seemed not only sufficient but more polished: the first murder on scene is in the nature of a prologue, and the final scene between Ellery and Seligmann in Vienna is in the nature of an epilogue.

(2) I call your attention to the words "Remember that" somewhere, as I recall, on page 2 of the outline. Here is an all-revealing clue, given to the reader in the very first chapter. It tells the reader that never in all the series of murders was the killer seen; yet, at the end, Cazalis is seen attempting the tenth murder. If the reader recalls "Remember that" in the first chapter, the reader will know that Cazalis cannot be the real murderer—the author said so in Chapter one by warning the reader that the murderer was *never* seen in the act of committing any of the murders. I like this device, and I don't think it is dangerous at all; if anything, it is challenging and provocative—even if the reader remembers the direct warning given by the author at the very beginning of the novel.

(3) Note that characters throughout the story are constantly being placed in circumstances that bring out latent violence. Jimmy becomes violent with rage at Ellery; Celeste becomes an enraged tigress. All this to sow seeds in the reader's mind: which is the insane killer? Of course, the two outbursts of near-violence on the part of Mrs. Cazalis are even more important plants—as referred to and explained by Ellery at the end. This susceptibility to rage and violence on the part of all with the significant exception of Dr. Cazalis—always, of course, as the result of specific stimuli—has strong psychological meaning; besides, it keeps adding to the tension and develops the thread of hidden mania.

(4) Ellery's suspicion that Jimmy or Celeste, or both, have taken advantage of Ellery's coming into the case to become an ally of the Killer's chief opponent is the beginning of a bluff and double-bluff motif. Here is the psychological pattern: Ellery's suspicion of Jimmy and Celeste will be discounted by most readers, especially when Ellery finally concludes that they are both as innocent as babies (always, by the way, references and cross references to babies on the one hand and to cats on the other). This will lead the reader to suspect that *someone else* has done the same thing—become Ellery's ally. Who will the reader pounce on? Dr. Cazalis. That is the "bluff." I don't think many readers will go past Cazalis to the real truth—that it was Mrs. Cazalis who became Ellery's ally—indirectly. Mrs. Cazalis represents the "double-bluff." And for a certain type of wise reader, there is an additional "double-bluff." Some readers will be certain that Ellery's conclusion that Jimmy and Celeste are innocent only points that more strongly to Jimmy or Celeste.

(5) Never have anyone call Mrs. Cazalis by a first name throughout the story. Her husband can always use "dear" or "darling" etc. when talking directly to her in dialogue. All others call her Mrs. Cazalis. I like this point very much. It heightens the final revelation of the true murderer as unknown, invisible, yet ubiquitous, ever-present.

(6) I call your attention to the perfect appropriateness of the final sex motive being revealed in Vienna, the home of sex motivation (and Freud).

(7) The day after I mailed you this outline Bill and I went to the movies—and saw *Naked City*. If you haven't seen this picture, try to catch it—because of its pictorial treatment of New York City as the background of a murder investigation. Actually, I did not know of *Naked City* at the time I was working on this novel. But *Naked City* will suggest many small touches: whenever Ellery is on a New York City street, background him with typical New York City sights—children playing, the roar of the El above him, etc.

(8) Before I forget, and this is a general observation: nearly everything I put into the outline had either a plot purpose or a psychological purpose. If in doubt, ask me.

(9) Another thought: suggest to publishers eventually to have a map of Manhattan drawn, with X marking the spots of the murders, and use the map as end-papers for the book.

(10) I made the serious suggestion that you deliberately write the story in a simple style—deliberate understatement, to enhance by contrast the background of terror, and so on. The simpler the style, the more effective I think this story will be—and the more chance it will have as a magazine serial: this was very carefully planned: it has definite breaks as a two-parter (although as a 2-parter it would have to be condensed), as a 4-parter, and as a 6-parter.

(11) I note your worry as to the amount of research on psychiatry. For God's sake don't go overboard on the psychiatric end. It is not necessary for Cazalis to sound like a psychiatrist addressing fellow psychiatrists. I firmly believe that psychiatric lingo can be kept at an absolute minimum—enough to give authenticity and no more. The psychiatric ideas can be expressed for the most part—almost, I would say, entirely—in ordinary, everyday words—and be just as effective, if not more so to the average reader.

Well, that just about shoots my bolt. [. . .]

DAN

In the following letter, Lee writes with great clarity about the psychological underpinnings of his relationship with Dannay. It's tragic that such understanding couldn't be translated into behavior; it would have made life a great deal easier for both of them. But to keep working under such burdens is an accomplishment in and of itself. I'm reminded of Robert Christgau's lines about John Lennon and Yoko Ono: "Marriage doesn't match models of sanity; it accommodates two human beings with the usual quota of quirks and worse. This may have been an unusually neurotic relationship. But why do we always assume that neurosis must be defeated, transcended, escaped?" It needn't be, of course—whether the marriage is actual or only metaphorical matters little. The toll that neurosis takes, however, can be an exorbitant one, as these letters show.

July 5 [1948].

Dear Dan:

[. . .] It's no new experience to find that we level against each other almost identical charges; each has a deeply etched sense of grievance against the other and it takes similar forms. The trouble between us arises from chronic and festering causes going far back past the origins of our business association to our respective childhoods, both separately and where they happened to overlap. I have my own theory (probably wrong) about the psychological causes responsible for both our plights as adults; there's no point in even bringing it up, as you would probably disagree and in any event the causes are beyond us. But whatever your set of motivations was, it produced in you a powerful desire and need to dominate. Mine produced in me a more negative aspect of the same thing: a dislike of and a rebellion against being dominated. When circumstances placed us together, we clashed. To make the clash more serious, we had always—from earliest childhood—been rivals; childhood competition in play became, by direct extension, a competition of ideas in adulthood. More complications came in as factors when it became obvious that there were temperamental and social rivalries between us. We were jealous of each other—each one in different ways for different reasons about different things. What began as friendly competition wound up as active and bitter hostility. The whole set-up was packed with dynamite; and our history as a "team" is a series of explosions. Neither of us has helped the situation, probably because at base we each have a foul and quivering sense of inferiority, and in the other man we see the personification of what we unconsciously have feared might be, at least in specific aspects, a "superior." That's why neither of us can take adverse criticism from the other, no matter how expressed or implied. That's why often we see criticism of an adverse nature where none was intended.

The abortive and sputtering attempts we have made over the past twenty years to "come to an understanding" were doomed to failure not only because we have always been antipathetic but because we have not even agreed that there was a "cause." For many years, for instance, you denied—at least professed not to understand—my "emotional" approach to you and us. It is only in the past few years that I have begun to grasp just how much basis there is for that "emotional" approach—not merely on my side but on yours also. For all I know, you may still deny this whole thesis; or at least, insofar as it includes you. I can only say that I have had so many evidences of your emotional involvement with me—as God knows you have had of mine with you—as to make—and here I don't know how to avoid sticking my neck out—any other conclusion simply inconceivable to me.

Even though some new trimmings may appear here, this is essentially all old hat for both of us; there's hardly any point in going on with it. We have always been in—and we are in it now more than ever—an unhealthy, unnatural relationship. I think the only hope, if any exists, of a better-adjusted and healthier relationship lies in two things: each of trying to dig out the causes of his own neurosis as it applies to the other, and each of us being constantly on guard against reactions which stem from deep causes and have little or nothing to do with the specific issue, whatever it may be. It's a job which must be done by both of us if it is to have least chance of succeeding, and it must be done with relentless—I almost wrote the word "heroic"—honesty and self-examination. [. . .] You get sick *after* you open my letters; I get sick *before* I open yours. The mere sight of your handwriting on the envelope upsets me. The dread disappears if the contents of the letter should happen to be non-controversial. If they are controversial, the feeling persists for a long time; and it makes little difference what the controversy happens to be. I don't know how much or how little effect your relations with me have had upon your personal life; but I know what mine with you have had upon mine. I have been trying to fight this for some time now and I have made some progress, and for frankly selfish reasons; I want to save my marriage and achieve at least a little peace of mind and happiness in what's left of my life. Our "trouble" has had, and to a smaller degree still has, direct bearing, for instance, on my day-to-day attitude toward my children. Each of us has frustrated the other for twenty years of collaboration; it's small wonder that the frustrations have sought, and found, totally unrelated outlets. That's what I'm working to correct. Not that success in this will have any important effect on our relations—I mean basically important; the effect will be upon my relations with my family, with possibly the self-disciplines involved tending to dampen the explosive possibilities always under the surface of our intercourse. I'm frankly ready to settle for that.

* * *

[. . .] In relation to you, I haven't even expressed what has happened to me. Since you bring it up, I'll discuss it. For whatever psychological reasons, since early in our collaboration something in me, or something in you, or something in us as we reacted to each other, gave me deep and painful feelings of guilt. It is futile to go into how much of what I did caused these feelings, or how much you contributed to them and to keeping them alive. For my part, I know what I did and I know how you employed what I did to sustain your domination over me. What has happened to me is simply that I have "worked out" my guilt-feelings almost completely. If I did anything to bring them into being, I now feel that I have made up for them, and cancelled them. I think it was these guilt-feelings that largely paralyzed me or at least immobilized me and left me weaker than you when a clash occurred, or even at non-emotional interchanges; I think they bred in me that horrible feeling of dependence on you way above and beyond any normal balance of capacities in a relationship. Now I don't feel dependent on you in that way; I have found a new strength, or refound an old one. I no longer feel that I owe you my lifetime and beyond. As far as our working relationship is concerned, I know my own capacities and their value to our collaboration; I am your partner now, and not, as I felt for so long, your creature. As your partner, I will give you what a partner should give, more or less; probably more rather than less, I being what I am; in any event, I think my contributions will balance off to what they should be.

All this is what I meant by "standing on my own feet." I might have said, "no longer standing on yours." If you're still standing on your own feet, that makes two of us; and I take it that's the preferred position for collaborators. [. . .]

Your last paragraph: "Right now I can look twenty years work in the face and ask myself: Do I know a goddam thing about what I'm doing? You tell me." All right, I'll tell you. For the greater part of those twenty years you knew, or thought you knew, exactly what you were doing. If now you find you must ask yourself that really horrible question, it may console you to learn that I have asked myself that question, not in the twentieth year, but in practically all twenty of those years. If you now have your own state of mind to judge by, you may be better able to judge how I've been floating around in the void—would Dante's Inferno be a better figure?—for what is actually almost half a lifetime. I never knew a damn thing about what I was doing, and do you want to know something? I still don't. All I can do is go ahead and work, and hope for hope, if not for something more tangible. [. . .]

This letter has taken the best part of the day and rather than hold it back until tomorrow, I'll wind up now and write you about the outline then. I'm mailing this now. So that there will be no further misunderstanding about this, I'll say here that I think you struck an interesting idea and you worked it out ingeniously. The difficulties I foresee are largely in the writing. On the negative side, because of the nature of the solution I don't think there's a chance of a serial; and I think there is a very good possibility of a movie sale if the criminal's motivation is changed.[. . .]

MANNY

July 7, 1948

Dear Dan:

About the novel.

There really isn't much for me to write. I like the idea a lot and, while on first reading certain things disturbed me, on re-reading I find them not disturbing me, or most of them. [. . .] The reason I said I didn't think this was a magazine serial is as follows: The nature of the solution, in both sections. I don't believe magazines will go for stories which turn out to rest upon a father killing his own children at birth and/or a wife killing innocent people who had been brought into the world by her husband for the reason that he has given babies to other women and not to her. I hope I'm wrong.

It strikes me, too, that—and I speak here purely from the magazine-serial standpoint—if magazines want in their stories central characters we care about, this story will be—from that standpoint—peculiarly wanting. We may care about Celeste and Jimmy in one sense, depending largely on what I do with them, but neither is so deeply involved in the overall problem of the story as to become the foci of our concern. [. . .] We are *concerned* with two people in this story: one is Ellery, and the other is New York City. As the detective, Ellery will arouse the reader's concern only to a certain degree; in any event what I think the magazines look for is not concern about the detective. As for the City, while a great deal can be done to personalize it, it still remains a vague entity and does not and cannot arouse the feelings in a reader that an individual can.

None of this is to say that the story won't be a good and interesting one; it is merely to say that I don't have the magazine hopes for it that apparently you had. As for movie possibilities, I believe they are pretty good—although, as I wrote you, I think the crime-motivation would probably have to be changed for a movie version. There is still the Johnson office and the Catholic Church. As a story of terror it has movie meat in it; you obviously had the movies strongly in mind when you did it.

I like the title, but I'm not sure I like it for this yarn. [. . .] I myself would infinitely prefer a much simpler title, with I think more graphic and more appealing properties:

The Cat

It is more direct, it is more pertinent to the subject matter, it sums up the terror, and it has a grim simplicity which—maybe it's a personal quirk—appeals to me far more than *Off With His Head*! [. . .]

I am a little disturbed by your appellation of Dr. Cazalis as "the greatest psychiatrist in America." The chronology you give him hardly fits in with that appellation. It takes long years of study to become a psychiatrist, and longer years of actual casework, usually in mental hospitals—neurological work, etc.— before a man feels himself qualified to set up in psychiatric practice. Granted Cazalis was a famous obstetrician or gynecologist, even a genius, the amount of years you have provided for his training, practice, and retirement is, in my opinion, inadequate to justify the psychiatric crown. I would very much like to see, if it can be done, a much longer period devoted to Cazalis's training and practice in psychiatry. [. . .]

While I'm thinking of it, I would like to express at this time a feeling I have which has arisen directly from *Ten Days' Wonder* and this one. And that is that we return, in the book following this one, to an Ellery who is not so chaotically upset by his case. I mean, you can push a good thing so far, then it ceases to have its original value. It is the kind of humanization of Ellery which I think is strictly limited, and I feel that with this story the limit has been reached. I would like to see him get some of his self-esteem back in the next one!—and incidentally, banish the uneasy feeling I feel sure will exist in many readers' minds that Ellery is "slipping." He's castigated himself enough. In the next one he ought to have a feeling of grim satisfaction, a very real triumph, with no ifs ands and buts.

The baby has been sick for a week and Kaye and I are going around with our eyes hanging out for lack of sleep. We think it's teething, but he's been running temperatures up to 103-1/2 daily and he's been on sulfa and hell knows what else, and he's acted like the worst brat in creation. We're relieved to hear that Steve's circumcision came off so well and I'm sure from now on in you'll have only the normal anxieties. For heaven's sake don't you and Hilda generate the psychology—in either yourself or him!—that he's "different" from other babies—except in the most normal sense. Regards–

MANNY

July 8, 1948

Dear Man:

[. . .] There has never been a day in these twenty years that I have not questioned my work, my ideas, my ability, my everything. Every piece of work I've ever done has been born out of doubts, misgivings, fears, anxieties. If I wrote you a fifty page letter, I could not begin to tell you the tortures and anguish I suffered with, for example, *Ten Days' Wonder*. At the end of every job I am sick as a dog—because I am sick before the job and sick during it. I am sick as a dog right now, as the aftermath of *Off With His Head*! and as a prelude to doing two issues of the magazine. I have never written even a half-page of editorial comment for a story in the magazine without suffering through every damned syllable. How little you know me. If you want a fairly accurate idea of what I go through, ask Hilda—she is just beginning to understand, and she gets the dirty end of it, before, during, and after every job I suffer through. Man, I often wonder how in God's name I ever manage to finish anything at all, how I manage ever to get anything on paper—on every sustained job there are a hundred times when I am ready, eager, and willing to give up. Does that sound like a superiority complex? [. . .]

I don't think, Man, that the nature of the solution rules out, or even hurts, the possibility of a magazine serial. The slicks have been using more and more so-called psychiatric motivations; they are not anywhere near as hidebound as they used to be. I think that if the rest of the story got them, they would accept the "psychological" motivation which comes out only in the last installment. [. . .] I don't care what motivation a movie company would be satisfied with, but I do care what motivation *we* would be satisfied with. An ordinary motive—like sheer insanity, and that's all—would not satisfy me. This story demands, I think, a deep and credible psychological motive. Indeed, it was the motive that put me through hell. It's all well and good to work out a series of murders; they may look indiscriminate and senseless and meaningless; but in the end they've got to be tied together by positive motivation. I'll admit that the motivation I worked out has a definite horror about it—a doctor murdering his own children in childbirth is shocking—but not only is it perfectly credible but it is in keeping, in tone, with the sense of horror and terror built up throughout the book. The touch of horror in the final revelation of motive will hit the reader hard; it has a memorable and significant quality—which I think is all to the good. [. . .]

Steve is having a hard time of it. The circumcision has disrupted his habits—eating, sleeping, everything. He still suffers pain, and while the healing is noticeable, it is a slow process. We think the kid lost weight this week, and we are anxiously watching him for a return to normal. He sure takes after me—always-the-hard-way. No more long letters, except in necessary discussion of the new novel. That's a promise—not only to you but to me.

DAN

July 9, 1948

Dear Man,

I have your letter of July 7 and we are all sorry to learn that the baby is ill. We hope that all is well by the time this letter reaches you. Steve has also been definitely under the weather. The circumcision was evidently a difficult hurdle for him. We had a doctor in last night, and the doctor admits that the little fellow was hit hard. It will be a week tomorrow since the circumcision, yet Steve is not yet back to normal in either his eating or his sleeping. He cries considerably more than usual, so it is possible he still has bouts of pain. [. . .]

No, we don't treat Steve as "different"—except in this [sic] physiological ways that the doctor tells us to. It will take about a year, nevertheless, for Steve to catch up in all ways. He's a most interesting little guy, partly because in some ways he is his full age and in other ways he's only a month or so old. He'll be four months old the middle of this month, and in that respect he's just as positive-minded a kid [as] you've ever seen. He knows what he wants, when he wants it, and wild horses can't budge him. He's very high strung—a bundle of nerves, the doctor says. (Hell, he's my son, isn't he?—stubborn and hair-triggered). The least change seems to affect him, and he undoubtedly has my nervous stomach.

Let us know that things are well with all your brood.

* * *

About your comments on the new book: as a matter of fact, I am delighted with most of them, and was hoping you would say some of the things you did say. [. . .] I have already written you about the nature of the solution and its possible effect on magazine serialization. Don't forget that the solution as regards killing-of-babies is just that: a solution. It is not the continuing theme of the story; it comes out only at the end. I remember that Paul Gallico once wrote a magazine story based on the killing of babies at a baby farm—you know, the kind of place where illegitimate babies, and babies not wanted for other reasons, are sent for upbringing. The magazine published the story although, as I recall it, the farm land was literally filled with baby corpses. If a magazine likes the main thread of the story, I think they would accept the motive which is brought out only at the end of the story. I could be dead wrong—I hope I'm not.

Yes, there are two main characters in the story—you are perfectly right. The main characters are (1) Ellery, and (2) New York City. This was deliberate on my part—I planned it that way. One reason was to give Ellery more than a deus-ex-machina status, to give you a chance to deal with Ellery more as a human being than as a detective-thinking-machine. I think Ellery has a deep human interest role in this story; he carries the fearful responsibility of the police—the responsibility is concentrated in him as an individual; he carries on his shoulders the terror of the whole city. Now, what is wrong with Ellery and the City being the main character? Forget that Ellery has twenty years of being known behind him. Think, for a moment, of this story as being the first one about Ellery. Why shouldn't a magazine find in the Ellery of this story the kind of character they want as a protagonist? Why can't the Ellery of this story be a real hero-character, enlisting the deepest sympathies of the reader?

True, Ellery is not in love with any woman; he carries no romantic thread. But is this necessary? Some of the most successful magazine characters are the human, sympathetic bystanders who pull the strings. I agree, however, that magazines do expect a romantic thread. This why Celeste and Jimmy are in the story the way they are. Granted, they are secondary characters, but even though they are secondary, they are strong enough for the necessary romantic thread. Plus, the fact that Ellery is the one who brings them together, breaks them apart, and finally brings them together again. [. . .] And don't forget the City: sprawling, diffuse, huge as it is, it is still a "character"—a background that lives and breathes, that has all the fears and feelings of a single human being. [. . .]

As to the motivation hurting movie chances, I wrote you about this too. The movies can change the motivation, if they want to, or think it necessary or advisable. A change in motivation never stopped a movie [studio] from buying a story before—at least, not that I know of. Give the movies the real meat of this story—the multiple murders, the vast City in mortal terror, the increasing tension, the love affair (with obstacles) of two young people who have been indirect victims, and above all, the single, sympathetic figure of Ellery carrying the whole load on his shoulders, single-handedly fighting the danger and the terror. [. . .]

I wasn't bothered about the length of time in which Cazalis could become "The greatest psychiatrist in America"; but if it bothers you, I see no harm in either (a) not making the greatest, but, say, one of the most brilliant, or (b) increasing the length of time for him to achieve the highest position in the field. You can do the latter by making him even older—though I liked the 65 age I finally gave him. If you change the number of years in which Cazalis trained and practiced as a psychiatrist, be very careful to check, and cross-check, and double-check all the possible implications—the relative age, for example, of Mrs. Cazalis, the relative age of Professor Seligmann, the whole chronology of Cazalis' background, the relative ages of the victims, and so on. A change of this sort, you will find, has ramifications throughout every phase of the story. I had to work very carefully to keep all the threads not only accurate but always credible. You'll have to be even more careful, if you make a chronological change of any kind—it will affect nearly everything in the story.

I agree with you thoroughly that after two books Ellery has had his full deflation, and that this type of humanization has been, at least for the time, exhausted. [. . .] I started it [in] *Ten Days' Wonder* and continued it in *Off With His Head!* as a deliberate means of flesh-and-blooding Ellery by deflation of his ego and of his mental prowess. I think, Man, that it will have served its purpose for the good, and that Ellery can succeed next time without any strings attached. But don't get the idea that in the last chapter of *Off With His Head!* (even including the tag line) Ellery is just a pricked balloon. The great man still pulls rabbits out of his head. Don't forget that it is Ellery, not the psychiatrist, who gives the reader the analysis. Ellery's brain is still there—it is only as an ego and as a human being that the case in general and Professor Seligman in particular pulls the chair out from Ellery, giving him one of the most artistic pratfalls ever handed a fictional detective-mastermind—a devastating one-two punch, the left thrown in *Ten Days' Wonder* and the right crossed in *Off With His Head!* Okay, Ellery gets up off the floor and in the next story comes back to win full honors.

Goddammit!—another day killed. But this letter was important. I am tremendously heartened by the chance to answer the particular queries and comments you made. I have a deep feeling that once you sink your teeth in this book, you are going to really enjoy working on it—and that is of colossal importance.

All our best,

DAN

July 29, 1948

Dear Man:

[. . .] About the Christmas story, duly received: Man, I would like tremendously to have a long talk with you about these shorts, but I realize it simply can't be done in a letter. It's too dangerous, as we have both discovered, to attempt back-and-forth criticism by letter. Yet I cannot go to the other extreme and say nothing at all.

I do think the story is too long—not too long *per se*, but too long for the story's own good. I have made a few cuts—mostly in pages 30 and 31 of the present ms; I would like to have made more cuts, but didn't feel that I should. [. . .] I honestly think my cuts help the story a little, as I think further cuts would also help the story—tighten it. However. I know perfectly what your approach to this series of stories is and in principle I approve without reservation. But I wish you would seriously consider the following suggestion: underdo rather than even risk the possibility of overdoing.

Specifically, as to the Christmas story: in all honesty, Man, I think the story is almost buried under the whimsy. [. . .]

* * *

As soon as I catch up to date with the magazine work, I suppose I must begin to think of another novel—we simply must reestablish ourselves without let-up. It's a frightening prospect on my part—I haven't the slightest idea, or germ of an idea, to work on—a complete blank slate. Plus the fact that I must do something altogether different from *Wonder* and the novel now in your hands— different in all ways. God knows how long it will take me just now to get on the track . . . Give me your thoughts on your own work schedule—on the new novel, I mean, with due regard for slicing in the remaining shorts. When do you think you can have the new novel finished? It may be important to have a deadline date by which to guide ourselves—so that I can give myself some sort of deadline on the next novel, so that [Little, Brown] can know when to expect, and so on.

We are all quite well, although we could use a vacation the way we could use more money. All our best,

DAN

Saturday July 31 [1948]

Dear Dan:

[. . .] Whimsy is one man's meat and another man's poison. For the most part I have found the whimsy in these stories nourishing; for the most part, apparently, you have found it toxic. So there we are.

But I began to speak of the peculiar circumstance of your editorial position. Naturally you would view the story as you view other stories coming into the mag—as a mag piece, from the mag editor's viewpoint. But none of these stories has been written for *EQMM* or for any other magazine, for that matter. The fact that they're running in *EQMM* is an exceptional circumstance. From the beginning I had in mind almost exclusively what these stories would read like when collected in a volume in chronological order. I have taken liberties with style and approach I would never have dreamed of taking had at any time a serious consideration been sale to a magazine first. [. . .]

As long as you're running the magazine I won't question your right to dictate what goes in and what stays out, for whatever reason. As one-half of Queen, however, and responsible for the writing of these stories, I do reserve to myself the right to say I would rather have the story excluded from the magazine altogether than trimmed or edited to make it conform more closely to your *editorial* view of what it ought to be for *EQMM*, when we are in disagreement about the trimming and editing. If in a case of submission to *EQMM* you must by the nature of the situation act chiefly as *EQMM*'s editor, by the same token I must act chiefly as Queen-the-submitter-of-the-story. [. . .] You are obviously very unhappy about "The Dauphin' Doll". Dan—and I say this with no rancor, no bitterness, and not the shadow of malicious intent—why don't you yank the story? In fact, I would prefer it. And then I could proceed with the other stories on an out-and-out book basis without any worries at all as far as you and *EQMM* are concerned. Of course, you would never like the resulting book; but you'd never like it in any event, so that's not a factor. I think both of us are fairly reconciled to the fact that his "collaborator" will consistently be unhappy about the results of his own contribution to the joint product.

* * *

One thing more before I leave this particular subject, I hope, for good. In view of the fact that your general dissatisfaction with the calendar stories has more or less come out, I think you ought to know just how I feel about them. I like them immensely, I have had a lot of fun doing them, I think they're highly enjoyable stories from a reader's standpoint and I think they will make an unusual book of short stories . . . "off the trail" in the non-opprobrious sense. I think it even possible that the book may get good reviews. Since you know and I don't what *you* think about them, you're now in a position to judge just how wide the gulf separating our judgments of them is.

* * *

You ask for my thoughts on my own work schedule. They are vague, which I know you will be unhappy to hear, as I am to have to report them so. I simply can't tell in advance, or plan in advance, how long a novel will take me. I am allowing myself a maximum of three months. I think two and a half months may do it. I will try to do it in two. Specifically, a miracle might find it ready by

October 1; the chances are it will be ready by October 15; but don't count on it before November 1. If this is as unsatisfactory to you as it is to me, we will agree on at least one thing on the current agenda. As to radio, I understand and sympathize with your complaint that you hear nothing about it on your end. What I have heard about it on my end is exactly what I have written you— neither more nor less.

Regards to the family –

MANNY

The following letter refers to "The President's Half Disme" and "The Inner Circle", two short stories that were later included in the collection *Calendar of Crime*.

August 3, 1948

Dear Man:

[. . .] I must say, Man, that you are tremendously illogical at times. For example: because I say that I would like the short stories much better if you made certain changes, particularly in balance, you conclude that I do not like the short stories at all. By no stretch of logic does this follow—except that you want it to follow. The simple truth is this: by and large I do like the short stories; I would like them even more if you happened to agree with me on certain points to the extent of making some of the changes I suggest. [. . .]

To show you further how deliberately you choose to misunderstand: you say that I do not like the short stories at all. Here is the evidence: I selected "[The President's] Half Disme" for the MWA anthology; I saw to it that the "Half Disme" was included in the Cooke anthology of the Best Detective Stories of the Year, to be published next month; I selected "The Inner Circle" for *Twentieth Century Detective Stories*, for which (as you certainly must concede) I selected stories only with the most fanatical care.

Or do you think I don't give a damn what comes out in anthologies or in *EQMM* bearing the Queen name? Is it possible that you think I am capable of publishing what I consider inferior work just for the sake of having Queen's name in a book or magazine, or for the few bucks the stories earn through anthology fees? All I say is what I said in the beginning, and have said all along: I could like the stories even more. As to a discussion of whimsy, pro and con, I simply won't be drawn into that! [. . .] As to the remaining stories to be written, I am assuming that you will arrange your schedule so as to meet *EQMM* deadlines. We cannot afford to lose a single date—not because of the money, but because it would require waiting a full year to make up any lost date.

There is one subject, Man, that with all my heart I do not want to discuss—and that is those rights you keep referring to as mine by sheer virtue of the fact that I do the editing of *EQMM*. Why not just give me credit for editing *EQMM* as sincerely as I know how? All I do on the Queen stories is make an occasional deletion. You ought to see what I do on stories by other writers!!! I have done one hell of a lot of re-writing on the others—including the best of them, by reputation and otherwise—and, Man, I have improved many a story, as the original authors usually concede, and I have saved many a story, as the original authors have also conceded. There is nothing personal, even in the most infinitesimal degree, in any changes I make—either in Queen stories or in others'.

On the new novel: [. . .] I'll keep you informed as to my progress. I will feel that I have jumped the biggest hurdle when I can write you that I have finally hit on a basic idea for the next novel.

We are all as well as the heat out here permits us to be. Steve is teething, and of course he picked the hottest spell—the kid just does everything the hard way. Hereditary, no doubt. Our best,

DAN

August 4 [1948]

Dear Dan:

I have been studying the outline, familiarizing myself with it, and certain things begin to stand out to me.

(1) There are nine actual murders in the story, and a tenth fake attempt by Cazalis. Your story of the city's panic explodes after the 7th murder—the scene at the Garden, etc. To warrant the scope you give to the panic, not merely at the Garden, but all the incidentals you put in describing the reaction of the city as murders mount in number, I am becoming convinced that there are not enough murders. It would take, I think, a lot more than 7 murders, no matter how mysterious, to whip a city like New York into a mass-exodus type of panic. I know you restricted your exact number of murders to 9 to round out the cat symbolism, but I think this can be discarded as the least important factor—certainly it can have no roots in the killer herself; as far as she is concerned, the fact that she was able to commit only 9 murders—carrying out the cat symbolism—can hardly be construed as anything but a coincidence. It's the author's symbolism, not the character's. I suppose it might be possible to project onto Mrs. Cazalis the symbolism, too—the papers calling her the cat gave her the idea, etc.—but it seems to me this would be weakening the main line of her criminal activity; if she's off her nut and is moved to kill the babies her husband brought into the world, she's not going to stop at 9, symbolism or no symbolism. [. . .]

(2) In the 9 murders actually committed, 6 are females and 3 are males. If the tenth victim-to-be is taken into account, it makes it 7 females and 3 males. I think this is inadvisable. The probabilities lie in exactly the opposite kind of proportion. As you point out, females change their names by marriage. So in hunting down Cazalis's cases chronologically, Mrs. C., who has no ax to grind and shows no favorites, but takes them as they come, would be bound, by the law of averages, to find more male names in the directory than female names. [. . .] The only conceivable purpose you could have had in mind, as I assume the preponderance of females was not an accident, was that more women being murdered than men makes it somehow more magaziney—with the added implication, perhaps, that with most victims being women, there may be something sexual in the murderer's background and that would tend to make the reader think of killer-as-male. If this last was in your mind, I don't think, in practice, it will work out. It will be absolutely impossible for me to write this story without at least touching upon, no matter how delicate and briefly, the possibility that these are sex crimes. (In real life, murders such as these would be construed, at least hypothetically, as possible sex crimes as their first theory by the regular police.) [. . .]

I suggest this: I suggest that the first murder be of a woman, so that the impact to the reader is woman-murder. [. . .] The only reason I can see for your having made your first victim a male was that it coincided better with your idea that the first victim should be a complete nonentity, a Mr. Nobody, and we associate maleness with that rather than femaleness. On the other hand, a female *could* be a Miss Nobody and it might even have a more pathetic quality. [. . .]

(3) This is a query: (I'm skipping around, mentioning these as they occur to me — What did you have in mind about the fact that, with the arrest of Cazalis, Mrs. Cazalis ceases operations? You mention that two months pass between Cazalis's arrest and Ellery's picking up the clue that leads him to question Cazalis's guilt. In that two months no other murders were committed—in fact, with Cazalis's capture the murders stop altogether, for good. Was it your intention to make this a frame-up? That is, that Mrs. C. was framing her husband out of revenge in her insanity and naturally stopped operations when Cazalis was put where he couldn't theoretically commit any "more" murders? Or that, her husband having been taken for the crimes she committed, a cunning born of her mania prevented her from doing another job? What did you conceive as Mrs. C's thinking on this question? [. . .]

(4) The question of Cazalis's chronology: It still disturbs me, the more so since I note what I had apparently skipped over before, or it hadn't registered: that you said he begun *practice* at the age of 21. To have done this, Cazalis would have had to be a boy prodigy. Today, of course, all recognized medical schools require 4 years of pre-med, the medical course is 4 years, and there is the minimum legal requirement of 1 year's internship—9 years in all. I believe

at the time Cazalis would have begun studying, the pre-med required was only 2 years. Even so, this would have represented a minimum of 7 years from time he entered college before he could possibly have set himself up, legally, in general practice. Meaning he was no older than 14 when he entered college. [. . .] I think the idea of an ultra-bright, precocious student is okay and right in line with what should be established for Cazalis; even so, I think it would be better to up his age a bit, on this score alone. And I will have to do some fancy figuring to increase the number of years between his entering the study of psychiatry and his retirement. To prevent his becoming too old, it may be necessary to reduce the ages progressively of his victims—in other words, instead of the first victim being 44, he or she might be 39, or 40, etc.

(5) Are you absolutely set on the idea that Cazalis *did* murder his three babies? Suppose, for example, Cazalis was not painted as "the greatest obstetrician in America" but as simply a gynecologist; suppose the fact was that, in his own supreme ego, he had insisted on delivering his own children, as now; suppose he had blundered or been inept (or unnaturally nervous!) and through his error or ineptitude the first baby had died, and the second baby (it might have in this case to be reduced to two). There is still motivation for a nervous breakdown, isn't there? In this case, Mrs. C's own deterioration can be predicated on a much simpler and more direct (and possibly less strained-feeling) "background": her husband has succeeded in bringing thousands of babies into the world, perfectly efficiently; but her babies he had bungled and they had died: I'll kill every baby my husband brought into the world successfully for other women. [. . .] I think it is even possible that Cazalis didn't bungle at all! Wouldn't it make a clearer, simpler, less "iffy" story if Cazalis's sole error consisted of the fact that he insisted on delivering his wife himself? And what happened was that in both, or even in three cases, the babies were born dead. In other words—no other doctor would have done any "better." True, this removes the guilt-motivation on the part of the doctor as you have it; but the substitute for it could simply be that he suspected, or knew, or found out subsequently that *genetically* he was at fault; in other words, the babies were born dead not because as a gynecologist he had erred but because as the male progenitor he has imbued the embryos with the seeds of their destruction—a hereditary taint he communicated, or something. Here, again, the progression of Mrs. C's mania is unchanged; in her obsessiveness it is still reduced to: He couldn't give me any babies, but he made it possible for thousands of other women to have them; I'll kill them.

I'm not trying to replot your story. It's just that I feel uneasy about Cazalis's having murdered his own babies—and alternatives suggest themselves. If, after reading this, you still feel what you have is best, I'll stick to what you have.

The question you raise about your editing of *EQMM* calls for a reply. I have never accused you, either directly or to myself, of insincerity in the editing of the mag. Very much to the contrary! I know how much you have put into it, how important it is to you personally, and it has never even occurred to me that you have ever done anything but your honest best in relation to it. I am here talking of effort and character. As for your ability, I can't judge by personal experience—I can only go by the opinions of those who have been in an author-editor relationship with you, and of course on the fact that the magazine is the best in the field, about which I have never had any doubt whatever; and that, of course, is entirely your doing. Tony Boucher has told me that he and others who have first-hand knowledge of your editorial talents consider you a very fine editor indeed; one of the best. So I have never questioned your ability, either.

What I do question—and this may well be my bias—is your ability to "edit" anything I do, objectively. It isn't even as simple as that. With virtually everything I do comes the added complication that it is based on material you yourself supplied. So I question not only your ability to edit anything I do objectively, but anything you have contributed to it, too. How objective are you where your own work is concerned? It's so easy to say that one is "objective" where one's own work is concerned! But how true is it? How true can it be? Particularly in so ill-adjusted, emotional individuals as you and me? I don't see how you can separate yourself simultaneously into three individuals: the editor, the man who supplied the plot in the story submitted, and the collaborator who is in a completely maladjusted relationship with his partner and vice-versa. [. . .]

Dan, this whole question of the magazine is and always has been a source of great bitterness on both sides. We could go on for years raking it up, the reasons, the cross-purposes, the entanglements, and none of it would do a damned bit of good. Because all we do is justify ourselves, or try to. The truth of the matter is, irrespective of the merit or demerit of any given suggestion or objection from the other man, each of us jealously guards his individual contribution to the work and each of resents any encroachment on his work by the other. The mere fact of a disagreement raises instantly an argument or arguments in defense of what is disagreed with. There is no acceptance of criticism because there is no wish for criticism. There is wish only for agreement, which rarely if ever comes. This goes for both of us. Even if there is agreement, or approval, it is given grudgingly or, what is more the case, not at all or in a negative manner.

Oh, the hell with this. It's giving you another case of insomnia and me a head like a watermelon.

* * *

We may as well clean this up to the bitter end. The magazine has been a vast sore spot with me for years, I have had a tremendous resistance to it, as you must know; and what you have always known, aside from *EQMM*, I don't read detective stories. I haven't read one, aside from our own, for many years; what little time I have for reading I devote to subject matter far, far away. Considering all this, I was hardly in a position to pass an opinion about its contents. As for its editorship, I have already gone into that.

It is quite true that I have made little or no comment to you about the magazine of a complimentary nature. Surely you know why? I was too fucking bitter about it and about you. [. . .]

Couldn't you relieve yourself of a lot of detail by delegating some of the work? And don't you hang on to the work, and keep your finger squarely in every pie, because hard as the work is it's the only work you've ever done in connection with Queen that's given you any unalloyed pleasure? Isn't a lot of your pressure attributable to your reluctance to let anyone else give you any creative assistance? I'm just asking. Maybe I'm wrong about this, too. But you always gave me the feeling, when you mentioned *EQMM* and how, for instance, the contests were driving you nuts—even when you had troubles, and real troubles—you always gave the feeling that you enjoyed every bit of it—even the troubles. [. . .]

I don't minimize your work on the magazine. I respect it and I think you've done and are doing a fine job. But don't expect me to burst out gratuitously with such comments, Dan. Any more than I expect you to burst out gratuitously with such comments about anything I do. It would be wonderful if we both did. But we're both kind of grudgingly bitter about the other, aren't we? I've long since given up hope that it will ever be any different. And, by God, I thought you had, too. Maybe there's still hope, at that.

MANNY

[Handwritten:] *I can't start the actual writing until I hear from you, especially as regards the question of first victim's sex. I will fill in by going ahead with the April story, part of which is already done.*

August 7, 1948

Dear Man,

[. . .] Even though it is only a little over a month since I sent you the outline, it will be difficult for me to recapture all the reasons I had for reaching the various decisions I did in deciding why I did thus and why I did so. These decisions were in the making for a solid three months, and by the time an outline is finished, I am so heartily soaked and sick of the job, and so worn out mentally from having made multitudinous decisions, that I gladly drop the whole thing. Result: the million details which are so clear in my mind during the work (you know how I work: mostly from memory; I always have the complete story in my head, supported by fragments of notes, when I finally start the outline)—as I say, the million details which are so clear in my mind during the work, fly out of my head the very first moment I can release them. That release is what keeps my mind from bursting after a three month's sustained effort.

But I do want to caution you most seriously about one thing: I never make a decision on any point in a story through whim or impulse. Whether or not I can recall all my reasons now, I assure you that every decision had solid reasons behind it. If I chose one box rather than the other for, say, the opening murder-victim, I had definite reasons. I will grant that I often—very often—work by what could be called instinct. But what is instinct? Surely, by this time, instinct is largely the unconscious knowledge in me that has grown up as the result of training and practice in plot-making. I can *smell* a good idea, mentally speaking; I know by that combination of instinct-and-training whether an idea is good long before I have analyzed its pros and cons. And I have come to trust my instinct. And seriously and sincerely, I have found my instinct reliable.

Now, to your queries and suggestions: As to the number of murders: In my original plan for the story, I actually had in mind thirteen murders. I even had in mind a tie-up with the number thirteen symbolically; also, I planned to work out the number of chapters so that there would be thirteen. But when I started writing the outline, I found that too many murders raised two objections: one, the more murders, the harder they were to handle; some of the murders, even when off-stage, became cumbersome; and two, the more murders, the more feeling of melodrama—in the rather cheap sense. Too many murders can give a corny, pulp feeling to the story—which must be avoided at all cost.

I finally decided on nine crimes—not *because* of the cat symbolism. That came after the decision to make it nine—just as most of the cat-symbolism arose out of the material, rather than the material being dictated by the cat-symbolisms.

I did not think seven brutal murders, all obviously by the same Jack the Strangler, insufficient to panic a city. Seven apparently blind, mad, unpredictable murders in Manhattan are not a few—not when they occur as a series, with cumulative effect, fed by newspapers, radio, and so on. (Remember what a *single* Orson Welles broadcast did in New York and New Jersey?) However, if you still feel that nine murders and a tenth climactic one (even though thwarted) are not enough I have no objection to your adding more. I certainly would not go past thirteen altogether—even that may be too many from a melodramatic standpoint. But if you feel that thirteen are required, you might do something with the unlucky-thirteen angle. If, for example, the Marilyn Soames attempted murder, which more than any other in the story is on-stage, built-up, suspensed, were the thirteenth, the "unlucky" feeling would add even more terror to the preparations and the waiting for the thirteenth murder to occur. Ellery and the Inspector would not only be fighting a brilliant killer (so they think at the time) but they would also be fighting that aura of evil which superstitiously surrounds the thirteenth of anything. [. . .]

Also: Ellery enters the case now at murder 6. At the next murder Cazalis enters the story. There should be no great hiatus between these two murders—6 and 7. Once Ellery is in the case, Cazalis should also be in just as soon as possible. So, if you consider inserting any additional murders between the present #6 and #7, they should not be dealt with in any detail: they should be merely mentioned appropriately, so that Cazalis' entrance not be delayed.

Again, Man, I must caution you: you know that a detective story of this type cannot be changed arbitrarily. A change in numbers, sequence and chronology of the murders has terrific ramifications. Even a single added murder would affect everything said thereafter. If you add any murders, you must check and double-check every possible ramification: timing, ages, references, etc., etc. I had to be devilishly careful when I worked out the present pattern. I suggest that whether you add murders or not, you draw up a chart of all the murders, showing dates, ages, number of days between crimes, and so on. Otherwise, I'm afraid, you will be guilty of inconsistencies and errors, despite your best efforts.

As to the ratio of male and female victims: it is true that I did deliberately make most of the victims female—but this is not nearly as great a "stretch" as you think. The population of Manhattan is definitely weighted on the female side—as is every metropolis these days. But aside from all this: I see no harm whatever in a little stretching, and see tremendous advantages. More women victims is better for the story; better for the impact on the reader; better for the magazine possibilities; better for movies—in fact, better all around. Actually, I could work out half a dozen perfectly credible reasons why Cazalis' files turned up more women prospects than men—but I really don't think it is necessary to justify this point. [. . .] I started on this premise: the most important murders, the ones that have to make the greatest impact on the reader and the ones that represent the high spots in the plot—these most important murders should be of women. There is no doubt of this whatever in my mind: I not only feel it to be true emotionally and dramatically, but I know as cold fact that readers are more thrilled and interested in the murder of a woman than of a man. (One confirmation: when *EQMM* covers show a woman's dead body, rather than a man's, it always helps sales. We do not feel that every *EQMM* cover should show a female victim, but you will notice that we use women victims much more than men.)

Now, which are the most important murders in the story?

Not the first one (Abernathy's). The first murder is strictly in the nature of a prologue. [. . .] The reader does not yet know the significance of the murder, its overtones, its connotations.

The first important murder is the book is that of #6—because this is the murder which brings Ellery into the case, and this is the murder which climaxes the list given by the inspector, bringing out the series-effect, the growing terror, and so on.

The next most important murder is #7—Richardson—because this brings Cazalis into the story.

The next most important one is #8—Petrucchi—because this climaxes the Madison Square Panic.

And the last important one is #10—Soames—because this is the one most carefully built up on stage, because it is the climactic murder in the series, because it involves Celeste, and because it ends with the capture, seemingly, of the killer. To recap: the important murders are #s 6, 7, 8, and 10. Therefore, in planning the story, I promptly made all these four murders those of women. This is a fundamental necessity—I hope you see that, Man. It would weaken the story tremendously if any of these four murders, from the standpoint of impact on the reader and growth of terror, atmosphere, and drama, were not women. The main thread of impact is in these four murders—irrespective of how many others are mentioned in the story, or even dealt with on scene, including the very first one. [. . .]

I decided that #4—McKell, Jimmy's sister—should be a woman. I think it much better for the story that the hero (secondary) should lose a sister than a brother. Again, the emotional impact is stronger.

Also, #5—Philippe, Celeste's apparent sister—should also be a woman. The relationship between Celeste and her sister is far more effective, and interesting, as between two women than between Celeste and brother (or male cousin). The nursing background of Celeste (to say nothing of whatever of the type of person Celeste is—that is, her character) is more poignantly and more credibly brought out with an invalid sister. Further, the fact that our hero and heroine (to speak of Jimmy and Celeste in those terms) have a far greater bond if they both lost sisters to the maniac-killer, than if they lost brothers.

That now gives us six women victims out of ten. We must begin to assign male victims or lose all feeling of balance. [. . .] Once I had decided on the first victim being a man, I realized that a woman victim must come into the story quickly. [. . .]

With #1 and #2 settled, #3 could be a man—O'Reilly. This, as a matter of fact, was necessary on another count. It was mandatory to get over as quickly possible (in the first three crimes) that one male victim was single and the other married. [. . .] Seven out of the nine. Naturally, the remaining victim—#9, Katz (and I do hope you'll retain that name)—was made a male. Now, mind you, while I have given you specific reasons for this choice of sex all along the line, I still do not feel that the results are sufficiently off-balance to worry about. [. . .]

Should you decide to add murders, you can make the added victims male. This would not interfere with the present basic pattern, which I feel most strongly must be retained. [. . .]

As to Mrs. Cazalis' activities after her husband's arrest. This is *not* meant to be a frame-up. I do not see a frame-up at all in this type of story. Mrs. Cazalis' crimes are not deliberate and premeditated in the artificial sense of frame-up.

They are wholly emotional crimes—wholly so—and this, to me, does not jibe at all with any such notion as framing her husband.

Now, you certainly must grant that in her own peculiar way Mrs. C is a brilliant person—twisted, yes, but cunning as hell. She certainly is not dumb. Further, she did not commit murders in order to be caught. She did not want to be caught. So, when her husband is arrested as the Cat, Mrs. C must sit down and think things out. She is insane in one way, but she is sane enough otherwise to be able to think things out. She realizes at once that if she continues the murders, while her husband is in prison, it will only serve to establish her husband's true innocence—she knows that he has deliberately taken the rap for her. Once Dr. C's innocence is known, we are in the same position that Ellery finds himself in at the end of the book. The police (and Ellery), once convinced of Dr. C's innocence, will realize (as Ellery does, at the end) that Dr. C was shielding someone. Who? Only his wife—on the basis of the very deductions Ellery himself makes. Therefore, Mrs. C realizes that if she continues to commit murders, it will only serve *to point to her*. Now, what do we know actually happened? We know that in the two months after Dr. C's arrest, Mrs. C visited him, and that at the end of two months of visiting her husband, they committed suicide together. What does this suggest? That surely in those two months they talked everything over quite frankly—only a complete understanding between the two of them would lead to double suicide. What they talked about can be left to the imagination of the reader; Mrs. C, let us say wanted to go to the police and tell the truth—to free her husband; Dr. C dissuaded her, persuaded her to let him take the blame. Perhaps she threatened to commit another murder—to prove Dr. C's innocence. Dr. C would point out to her that that would not do any good; another murder would indicate his innocence but it would (as above) point directly to her, and to her alone. He could also threaten, if she committed another murder to prove his innocence, to tell the police that she did it only to save him—that he is still the Cat, that he had committed all the previous crimes.

So, they talked and talked. She realized that committing another murder, or more than one, would not really help. In the end they both realized what is implicit in the final revelation: that it was hopeless, not for one of them, but for both of them. Nothing either or both could do would erase the past, the already committed murders; further murders were useless—even to appease Mrs. C's mania, now that her husband is virtually doomed to execution. There was only one way out for them—for the two of them—and they took that way: double suicide. All this seems very clear to me. As I said, it is implicit in the very act they finally decided upon together. That suicide pact explains everything, including the complete halt in the murders. [. . .]

I do not see Cazalis as a boy prodigy. Yes, he is precocious, the youngest in his class, brilliant, and so on. But not a prodigy. Child prodigies, except in music, seem to wind up as missionaries—seldom, if ever, as brilliant men in later life. [. . .] As to the motive. I still think, Mon, that Cazalis' guilt complex should be as strong and easy-to-understand as possible. The fact that he killed his own three babies is not only a most unusual motive, but it is almost overwhelmingly powerful in its impact. I grant that, that when the reader is first told, there will probably be a touch of horror; the reader will probably shudder. But is that bad? [. . .]

To me the motive is tremendously interesting. It has enormous impact—which is not true of nearly all other motives in detective stories. Sheer over-use has taken the power out of greed, love, and all the other now-common motives. Here, on the other hand, is something new, something different—true, a shocker, but one which ties up all the elements in the story.

I still think, too, that if Mrs. C knew about her husband's killing their own babies, that their marriage could not possibly survive. I grant that their marriage survived despite Cazalis' conviction that she was unfaithful to him; many marriages have survived that suspicion—perhaps, most marriages! But I do not believe the same principle applies to Mrs. C. If she knew her husband's actions, she simply could not stand it indefinitely; there is no comparison between adultery and murder-of-babies-in-childbirth. The latter is monstrous—I do not think any woman could accept it.

Your counter suggestion that Cazalis did not kill his babies, that they died through ineptness or bungling, strikes me as weak in comparison with the stark, brutal truth now in the story. I wish you would think this over some more. I have thought it out a million times in the planning of the story, and always I am drawn back, irresistibly, to the power and impact of the proximate cause of the whole story: that Cazalis did murder his own babies in childbirth. Maybe, it's a highly susceptible or even a blind spot with me; I don't know anymore. But I feel that any diluting of this utterly convincing and utterly monstrous motive will lead to loss of strength all along the line—psychologically and emotionally.

As to the babies being born dead, because Cazalis was genetically at fault: I have the same feeling of weakened effect. It would certainly greatly weaken Cazalis' guilt complex, and I think his guilty phobia should be as strong as possible. True, you would substitute a subtler guilt complex, but the very subtleness strikes me as weaker and more difficult to get over to the reader and, if so, in the end less convincing. [. . .]

I think the present motive serves the story best, as a story and as a book. If, with the shocking and powerful motive, we fail to get a magazine sale, we might then ask the magazine if a change in motive would make any difference—but ask them only after they have read the finished story. If a change in motive would make the difference between magazine sale and rejection, the re-writing involved would only be in the last chapter. God knows magazines have often, if not most of the time, asked for changes before final rejection. I was told by Ngaio Marsh's agent that when [*The Saturday Evening Post*] was interested in her last book, for serial [. . .], they asked Ngaio Marsh for such extensive changes that she had to virtually re-write the book.

Why do you feel, as you expressed it, so uneasy about Cazalis having murdered his own babies? Do you recoil from the horror, the shock? If so, is that really bad? [. . .]

As to the movies: they would change everything anyway. I have never known of a movie sale being lost because a change was necessary in the last scene.

* * *

Well, I've tried to cover everything you brought up. If I have omitted anything, let me know. (I simply can't resist it: *And you want shorter outlines!*)

Too damned tired to say anything else—except that we are all fairly well, except me. [. . .] I am well aware, now that we are on a steady novel diet, that it's going to be damned hard on me. Actually, my work for the magazine is already down to essentials—yet I will have to work out some way of doing the magazine and the novels jointly. It's all well and good to say: delegate more work. Again, I ask: what the hell can I delegate?

DAN

In the following letter, Lee mentions Dr. Samuel Yochelson (1906-76), best known as the co-author (with Dr. Stanton E. Samenow) of *The Criminal Personality*. Later on in these letters, Lee writes of his desire to undergo analysis with Dr. Yochelson. Whether he did or not is unknown; we do know, however, that Lee (along with other members of his family) saw a psychiatrist after returning to the East Coast.

Monday Aug. 9 [1948]

Dear Dan:

[. . .] The fact that Cazalis murdered his own three infants doesn't "shock" me, it is not a case of horror, or bad taste, or anything like that. Let me see if I can't explain it exactly. I don't pretend to have any great psychiatric knowledge, but I have done enough reading to have at least a smattering of the fundamentals; and then, my association with Sam Yochelson for many years opened up to me the whole field and gave me a continuous awareness of those fundamentals by intimate contact with a brilliant psychiatrist. As far as I know, you are not as well informed as I on this particular subject—a fact that's neither to your discredit nor to my credit; I merely mention it because it lies at the root of this whole discussion. For purposes of your story, you had to have Cazalis cover up his wife or, at least, act the part of the mass-murderer when, in fact, he was innocent. [. . .] You came up with—"he killed his own three babies," giving him a powerful sense of guilt—an unusual motive, no doubt about it, and seeming to make it inevitable that he would, to expiate his guilt, assume the blame for the crimes that his wife, driven insane by her suspicion of the truth, had in fact committed herself. Or, at least, if not inevitable, then strongly plausible.

But when you came to weave it into your plot, you came—in my view—a cropper. You liked the idea so much (as you say in your last letter) and it seemed so powerful to you, that you let Ellery arrive at it without any factual basis beyond the disparity in the ages of Cazalis and his wife, all the rest being pure speculation—maybe plausible speculation, but certainly not exclusive of other speculations equally plausible. You postulate a possible jealousy on the part of Cazalis—plausible, yes; but suppose he wasn't jealous? You postulate "his wife's relationships...with other men, especially younger men"—not based on a single fact known to Ellery. How did he know Mrs. C hadn't been—as so many young wives of famous and brilliant men are—completely wrapped up in her husband and had no "relationships, no matter how innocent," with other men? How did Ellery know that Dr. C was *not* the type of man who goes "insanely jealous"? I would say, in fact, that judging from the character you have given him, he was too supremely egotistic a man to become jealous without cause. Or was there cause? *If* there was, where is the fact, or the indication? You postulate Dr. Cazalis brooding during the nine months of his wife's first pregnancy. Why? On what fact? Might he have brooded? Yes, but did he? I don't want to keep plugging this, but the point is that, by that type of hypothesis, choosing all along the line the speculation that adds to his pre-conceived thesis, Ellery reaches the "conclusion" Dr. Cazalis murdered his own three babies in childbirth. [Handwritten in margin by Dannay:] *The truth is, Ellery actually jumps to the conclusion that C murdered the babies and then "reconstructs" what must have happened—there is actually no deduction at all—it is pure inference based on guesswork.*

Dan, that's a very tall conclusion from mere hypothesis. The very thing about the conclusion that you like—its brutal starkness, its unusualness, its being so startling—makes it stand out so importantly that the reader must cry out, "For God's sake, how did Ellery arrive at *that*?" The trail of argument is thin, tenuous; at every point we could go off on a bypath, but Ellery didn't. Ellery of all people! [. . .] My point is that, in order to have Ellery arrive at the conclusion, or give the impression of having arrived at the conclusion, that Dr. C murdered his own three babies, it is mandatory, in my view, to give him facts to base his conclusions on, not merely speculations from possibilities. [. . .]

That's one part of my uneasiness. Another is this: [. . .] The fact is that Cazalis, a "world-famous psychiatrist," could probably have reasoned away any normal feelings of guilt if he had committed the crime much more easily than he could have adjusted himself to the decision to assume the burden of punishment because his wife had become psychotic through brooding over his crime. *Because, Dan, as a psychiatrist he would know that, even if he had not killed the babies, his wife would probably have become psychotic anyway!* Psychoses aren't *caused* by overt acts. Overt acts merely create the crises as a result of which the psychotic personality takes dominance. In other words, there was the psychotic personality to begin with, and for that Cazalis would surely know, as a psychiatrist, that he couldn't be in any way responsible. He would also know that sooner or later a psychological crisis of some kind would come along and his wife would "go over." We would have to know a hell of a lot about Mrs. Cazalis's childhood and bringing up (and we know nothing about it) to know what turned her potentially psychotic. If anything, I would say that the strongest motive implicit in the facts as you have them, for Cazalis to assume the guilt of his wife's acts, is that as a psychiatrist he didn't know, or knowing didn't do something about, the emotional disturbances that led her to commit mass murders! I'm not being in the least bit facetious or satirical.

In short, I not only feel that having Cazalis have murdered his own children, as you work it out, is technically suspect but is psychiatrically wrong and therefore not true. Or at least it raises a host of questions not even touched by your plot outline which anyone with a knowledge of the subject would spot and which, to that extent, weakens the story. And, frankly, I don't feel qualified to go into those questions, even if it were advisable that we did. I should have to go into psychiatric investigation with both feet, and I have neither the time nor the inclination for it. And you said it should be kept down to a minimum! Even if I grant that the average reader will be unconscious of all this and will accept what is written, I don't feel "easy" about doing it when I know it is open to severe criticism by those who are informed. It seems to me the simplest, safest, most all-around satisfactory course is to kill the idea of Cazalis's murder of his three babies. I can imagine, having read your letter, how difficult a decision this would be for you to make. If it were made, however, a substitute would have to be found to explain Cazalis's taking over the responsibility for his wife's acts. [. . .] *Because now, as you have it, the fact that Cazalis killed his own babies is so strong, so startling, so unusual that it quite overshadows the revelation of Mrs. C's guilt for the murders which took up the whole of the story to that point.* I don't believe you are conscious of how much out of balance that revelation makes the story. [. . .]

Frankly, Dan, on the basis of the past I don't have much hope that you will be able to see this my way to the extent of agreeing to a change. But I had to make my pitch in justice to the novel as I see it. If you arrive at the conclusion, no matter by what route, then, hell, leave it the way it is, I'll do my best to make it as plausible as it's possible for me to do.

Since I don't get to Cazalis for some time, I'll get going on the novel immediately. [. . .]

MANNY

August 13, 1948

Dear Man,

You say that when I came to weave the motive into the plot of the new novel that I came a cropper—that I let Ellery arrive at the solution without any factual basis—that Ellery's solution is all pure speculation—that Ellery's conclusion is very tall from mere hypothesis—that the trail of argument is thin and tenuous— Ellery of all people! [. . .]

From novel to novel, with never an exception, I am psychologically whipped and battered even before I begin. I face a million decisions: every single one of them is a mental road-block. [. . .]

Take this matter of Ellery's arriving at the solution without the usual kind of facts and the usual kind of Queen deductions. I thought I had made clear to you—in our phone conversation and in my letters—that I deliberately abandoned the Queen method of *The Chinese Orange Mystery* or even of *Calamity Town*. Time and time again I told you I was not doing a deductive detective story. [. . .]

Don't you see, Man, that what I gave Ellery—deliberately, I repeat—is a kind of mental magic. He spins his theories so plausibly that even though they are pure speculation, no more, they are utterly believable. Ellery starts from nowhere and gets somewhere. Ellery starts with nothing and in the end has everything. It is a trick, Man—an illusion—a wonder—a miracle. It is done with mirrors—mirrors of the mind. It is possibly a tour de force.

Maybe it didn't come off with you. I can't help believing that it didn't— otherwise, so long after the fact, you wouldn't be raising the question of facts, facts. Well, if it didn't come off, then I failed. Yet you yourself fell under the spell; you yourself were impressed by the plausibility. Don't you think that most readers—the tremendous majority—will not only find Ellery's solution plausible but also convincing? If that is so (and I think it is), then the trick *has* been pulled off—and without a single fact in the usual detective-story sense!

Ellery of all people, you say. Yes, Ellery of all people. Ellery without facts and deductions therefrom. Ellery working only with ideas, only with words, only with intangibles. Ellery working only with his brain—but instead of dealing with material clues, as heretofore, he is now dealing with people's thoughts, motives, actions, secrets. [. . .]

What would you want to do now? Add facts and deductions? Give Ellery his usual bag of tricks? Spot a clue there, and tie them up in the end with incontrovertible deductions? Manny, what I'm trying to do is get away from the old Queen Method which proves that X, and only X, could have been the culprit. [. . .]

I'm trying to get away from material clues and positive, ultra-logical deductions. Perhaps what I've got away to is even worse—obviously, I did not think so. But in the last analysis I have to do what is in me to do, just as you have to write what is in you to write. I thought I was doing something distinctive, something unusual—something different from what all the others are doing—something different, perhaps, from what all the others could do. And yet, despite this changing of both technique and attitude, I also thought that I was doing something that would have magazine possibilities. [. . .]

Because the new method is not as irrefutable as a mathematical formula, or a test-tube finding, what did I have Ellery do? Travel thousands of miles *to ask questions!* I repeat—*to ask questions*! True, Ellery could have been very apologetic in talking with Seligman, but I did not see Ellery that way. I see Ellery with a new strength, a new dynamic confidence in his theories and speculations—*because* they are based on people rather than cold facts. True, too, I have written to you that I agree the deflation period has run out—but I meant the deflation part of it, in the sense that Ellery first has to be all wrong, before he is right. In the last two cases Ellery has been "too late with too little." In the next case Ellery should not be too late with too little. But I would still like to see Ellery making conclusions from feelings rather than from facts.

And, boy, could I be wrong! Nevertheless, I have a deep faith in this approach. Now, as to the psychiatry angle. Man, what in the world do you expect me to say after you tell me, flatly and arbitrarily, that I am not as well informed on psychiatry as you. That makes any statement by me completely meaningless. You are no doubt correct; I have never studied psychiatry, nor been treated. On the other hand, Man, it would be equally true if you told me, in the same positive terms, that I am not as well informed as you on any of a hundred subjects. Shall I build stories only and exclusively out of what I know with exhaustive professional knowledge? If so, I could build little. [. . .]

If I get to the point where I must question every trait of character, question every action and reaction, I will spend three years on my end of a book instead of three months—and still get nothing done. I have to deal with people as I know them. [. . .]

Feeling the way I do right now, I must simply turn away from trying to find an idea for the next novel. I'll do some other work for a while. I don't feel that I could get anywhere on a new novel in the state of bewilderment and completely shaken confidence that you have put me in—on this last book as on all others, Man. I don't think you remotely realize to what fearful extents you tear apart everything I do.

We are all about the same. Bill and I need a vacation badly, but there is no way for us to get away even for a few days. The summer is virtually over, the boys will be going back to school soon, the grind goes on interminably, and I have a sadness deeper than can be explained by the passing of summer. [. . .] We hope you are all well. North Hollywood seems millions of miles away right now.

DAN

Wednesday Oct. 27 [1948]

Dear Dan:

[. . .] I wholly disagree about the magazine chances on this book, as I seem to remember (a century ago) I expressed doubt before, on that score. I can now talk from a direct knowledge of the finished or near-finished product and you, of course, can't. [. . .] It is easy to lose sight of the DIFFERENCE in your problems and mine. You can "order," as it were, a certain physical set of proportions, but most times I can't deliver. Because what you gave me to do in the various parts, and what I feel beyond that must be done to bring to life or make plausible what you gave me to do, forced me into certain things that put everything out of kilter ('kilter" being your kilter as per outline). The great difficulty to me (and a pleasure at the same time) in this job has been the very unusual job of handling the City, as—in effect—a character, or at least an overall and omnipresent background. I'm not talking about descriptions of places or neighborhoods or anything like that. By "City" I mean "People"—the people whose jitteriness and fear dominate the story and give it its importance. Without it there is very little, as we both recognize. [. . .] New York is a city of seven and a half million people, half of whom never see a newspaper or listen to a newscast. Murders, suicides, epidemics, God knows what, rage in New York all the time, and most people don't even know about it, except vaguely, and certainly it doesn't affect them one iota if they do—unless it happens to strike home or close to home. What was I to do? I had the further headache of realizing that *even the nature of the murders* was no real help in achieving the desired effect. I grant without argument that seven, eight, or nine murders MIGHT upset the whole City dangerously *if they were of a certain nature*. If they were horrible enough, for instance. If a series of murders occurred, each victim being found drawn and quartered, or beheaded, or deballed, or something, if enough savagery and bestiality were evident in the murderer, such an effect might be got. But obviously this was impossible. What the hell to do? I puzzled and puzzled over it. Because the more I thought about it, the more evident it became that unless I could make the reader see the BIGNESS of this murder series—that is, a reign of terror, as you put it—unless it WAS a reign of terror, the book dwindled instantly into the average class. [. . .]

I think I solved the problem, but to tell you how would take me almost as long as the solution itself. It involved no measurable addition or even alteration of material. It involved just plain goddamn writing. Of course, it may well turn out not to be as successful as I think it is, or not successful at all. I think, though, that it is.

HOWEVER. In solving this dominant problem—which I don't think you saw as such in doing the outline, or at least didn't see through to its actual difficulties—I have had to get away from the slick-magazine line. I don't think any magazine is interested in how the City of New York went berserk, and why. (DON'T get the jitters; I haven't enlarged your riot!) I think magazines want, still want, and always will want, stories of people centrally involved. Dan, this story is TOO GOOD for the magazines. When I say "too good" I mean just that. I don't mean too smart, or too profound, or too anything but that it's a study in mass mood, revealed through a rather off-the-trail style of attack. It is also too real. This is the first story I have worked on in which—with the exception of Jimmy and Celeste, who are still Hollywood—the people stand out as real people, not phonies. And I don't mean the "main" characters. There are really no main characters. Every character in it is, in a sense, a main character. We get the City through the people who are mentioned in it, the feel of its scope, its heterogeneity, etc.

I think, too, Ellery emerges—really for the first time—as a full-fledged character. A good beginning was made—from that standpoint—in *Ten Days' Wonder*. [. . .] I have done a lot of the feeling of the City's mood *through* him, without losing at any time (I don't think!) the always-present feeling that he has hidden powers that will eventually take over. Whatever it is that you're working on now, I BEG you to keep Ellery real and no inflated cardboard hero. It took twenty years to get him here, and I wouldn't like to see them blasted away. [. . .]

Oh, yes. This may or may not come to you as a surprise. This will be a long novel. I had no idea it was going to be. *Ten Days' Wonder* was short—takes only 260-odd printed pages. This is going to be its grandfather. DON'T get the shits. It can always be cut by the magazine that considers it, although if they do—again in my biased estimation—they will hurt it as a piece of work . . . It's as much a surprise to me as perhaps to you. You remember I said I thought originally it was going to be quite short. That was before I saw the difficulties at nose-point. You just can't skeletonize the City of New York! It's a big corpus . . . This news will probably come to you as the greatest blow of all. I know what stock you place on BREVITY—where I am concerned particularly! But then I can always point to the letter you just wrote me in which—granted an altogether different problem—you said you just couldn't keep the length down. Well, neither can I.

Of course, the greater length is slowing me up, too.

Whatever the result, by the time it's finished I'll know I've been in something LARGE.

GoodBYE!

MANNY

October 29, 1948

Dear Man:

I received your letter of Oct 27 last night, read it twice, and then waited for this morning. I have now read the letter for the third time, and I am just as ill as I was last night. [. . .]

If the cat story is less than average, without your particular treatment of the city-background (whatever your treatment may be) saving it from worse than mediocrity, then, Man, I simply must give up, if only to retain a sliver of self-respect.

If the cat story is less than average, from any viewpoint whatever, then, Man, I am in the wrong business and should go out and find myself a job as a mailman where I am told what to do, how to do it, and precisely what streets to walk on.

If the cat story is less than average, Man, then I have no creative ability whatever, I have no critical judgment whatever, never had any, never will have any, and have been fooling not only you but the public for twenty years, and after those twenty years of self-delusion and perpetration of fraud, have not even learned the fundamental ABCs of the detective story.

If you keep telling me that long enough, in one way or another, in one form or another, I'll wind up believing it.

For it all gets down to this, Man: as has happened in every other novel, we have reached that stage in the cat novel when you begin the process of (1) deflating the outline and (2) inflating the finished product. [. . .]

Look, Man: if the cat novel, viewed from any angle whatsoever, really were mediocre, if the cat novel has so little in it as you maintain, then I am getting my just desserts—and, damn it, I should be put in my place. But as I live and breathe, as I sit and make myself physically ill with every single book I work on, as my soul is my judge, I do not believe that what you say is true.

I have most of the first draft of an outline on the next novel finished. If I obeyed my innermost desire, my deepest impulse, I would take those pages of the outline and tear each and everyone one of them into a thousand pieces. If all the previous jobs are what you finally manage to say they are, then this new job is no better. [. . .] But there is one other aspect which I simply must bring up, and even ask you for an explanation. And that is your decision to treat the story in a non-magazine way, and [how] this affect[s] its potential earning power. [. . .]

Now, let us analyze our financial prospects. There are precisely two sources of income we can count on: one, the publication of two new books a year (maximum), and the income from *EQMM*. Nothing else is dependable: we cannot depend on radio, or reprint royalties, or anything else. [. . .] What is the obvious course? To try to get back into magazines. Therefore, I planned the cat novel with magazine (and movie) in mind. [. . .] What do you now tell me? That the treatment, the approach, the interpretation you finally selected *rules out* any possible magazine sale; and of course you tell me this when it is obviously too late even to discuss the matter.

Your decision was a crucial one. I do not even want to discuss the literary end of it; if you feel that you have the last word on the literary end, I can only agree. But when the last word on the literary end affects the financial end, don't you think you should have at least given me a chance to express my opinion? [. . .]

In view of your decision to treat the cat novel in such a way as to make magazine sale impossible (rather than, no matter how futile, still possible), I must ask you what kind of stories are we writing? What are we aiming at? Is potential income a factor or not? Is there any point in my having one approach and you having the opposite approach? How can I plan one way and you execute so as to obliterate even a vestige of chance? I am so confused, so utterly unnerved, that, believe me, I don't know where we are going.

What am I, in this terribly late stage, supposed to do with the book I am now working on? [. . .]

The new novel has no psychological conflict. It is basically what you yourself asked for: a return to the straight detective story, a return to the old Ellery. Yes, you yourself asked for that; now you beg me to keep Ellery real. [. . .]

This continual buffeting and battering—this continual deflation of my ego and, more important, my self-confidence—this continual sowing of disagreement and reaping of confusion—all this, Man, is reducing me to the state where one of these days I will not be able to work *alone*. Is that, Man, what you really have in mind? Is that what is behind your changing appraisals, your varying demands, your periodic inconsistencies?

The upshot right now is simply this: I am dropping the new novel—I don't want any part of it. I'll get back to it when I feel that my mind is clearer, when I feel I can exercise unwarped judgment, when I feel that I am not thoroughly beaten even before the story sees the light of day or your first reading of it.

If I could also drop *EQMM* at this moment, I would do that too. I wouldn't do a fucking thing that calls for thinking or planning or creating until I am completely out of my present frame of mind. But unfortunately I can't drop *EQMM*: there is the contest to wind up and deadlines to meet.

And unfortunately there are bills to pay. With which statement I come back to: How could you possibly have *ruled out* a shot at a magazine sale without first talking it over with me, without at least giving me some chance to plead for a magazine approach?

DAN

Wed. Nov. 3, 1948

Dear Dan:

So here we are again. I was up until almost 4 this morning listening to the election reports, fell asleep after 4. At 7 o'clock the front doorbell rang and I dragged myself out to get your special. Out here, or at least in the Valley, they never deliver specials after the day's regular deliveries, they wait until the next morning. Every special I have ever received from you has been delivered between 6 and 7 a.m.

So, headachy and bleary-eyed, I opened your fat letter and there it was, for the which time? Only this time I was really thrown. I went back at once to my correspondence with you and reread what I had written you. And, after reading the last two letters twice, I still don't understand fully what goes on here. All I can do is take up your letters—you really sent me a double header—point by point, kill the rest of today, and for what? To feed a fire that's apparently inextinguishable. And all on less than three hours' sleep. For of course it wasn't possible for me to go back to bed after reading what you'd written. [. . .]

Let me go through for you a little of my reflections. The usual story—let's say *Ten Days' Wonder*—no matter what its quality, still rests on certain common denominators. It almost always, for one thing, centrally involves a set of characters. This story (always in my view, of course) did not. THIS I LIKED. It was different. It had freshness. It opened up possibilities. Also difficulties, to me, at any rate. In no sense could Jimmy and Celeste be considered "centrally involved characters" in the normal, story-building meaning. They were involved characters, yes; but not centrally, in the sense that everything stood or fell by what happened to them. [. . .] Because the Jimmy-Celeste gambit took so little physical space proportionally in your outline; they actually came into the story in your outline so little; and much more importantly, because you had provided something in your outline that began smack on page 2 or 3 and went right through almost to the end without let-up: the reaction of these crimes on the city. In other words, as I saw it, as I saw no other way of seeing it, within my capacities, it was the City which served the usual function of providing the emotional counterpoint of your story, corroborated—even urged—by you in correspondence, and importantly Ellery had to catch the Cat in order to restore the City (not "characters") to the usual happy ending. [. . .] I dug in. What were the ingredients you had provided for the reign of terror? The mysterious murder of unconnected, apparently wholly innocent, New Yorkers.

Now your job, I repeat, was finished when you ordered reign-of-terror and indicated something of its nature and direction. My job was to take what you gave me and upon that build THE EFFECT THE STORY HAD TO HAVE IF IT WAS TO CARRY OUT ITS FUNCTION. [. . .] YOU had ordered BIGNESS—to put it in its most elementary way—BIGNESS (of the City-reign-of-terror motif) was an integral part of the story; AND UNLESS I ACHIEVED BIGNESS IN THE FINISH THE STORY WOULD BE UNSUCCESSFUL, JUST ANOTHER HACK-JOB FOR ITS MAJOR LENGTH. In other words, if it dwindled into the average class, it would be MY fault, NOT YOURS. [. . .] I suppose I'm expressing this badly, and maybe you still don't get it, but it's perfectly clear to me, and in any event, not one of your inferences from my letter is the case, not one; my remarks were directed toward my part of the job, not yours, and in no way was anything I said meant to be, or felt to be, a reflection on or a criticism of your outline. [. . .] It's a little ironical that what was meant to explain my attempts to make my part of the work live up to yours, was taken by you as an accusation that your part of the work stank and my part was to cover up the smell. [. . .]

Well, I'm way off, undoubtedly. I stink. I don't know this from that. I have lousy judgment and let myself run away with myself and I overwrite at times and I even get overenthusiastic once in twenty years and unquestionably I should be a typist in some office for $40 a week; but the fact remains this stuff is what I live on, this is my work, this is what I am spending my life doing, this is my contribution to society, this is what you're stuck with, this is what I live, breathe, sleep, eat, shit into the toilet every morning and have for twenty years, this is what's turned what hair I have left gray and made me an irascible maniac to my wife and children—and you talk to me about "final decisions" and "sole domain" and "affecting income" as if I were some cool master of finance sitting in my palatial office somewhere directing and manipulating destinies—including your own? You've made "final decisions" for twenty years that have affected my income as well as yours—yes, and in your sole domain. Every time you sit down to plan a story you make final decisions that affect our income. Why have you rights that I do not? What am I, some miserable hack who sits at a machine waiting for the master to throw a blueprint down? [. . .]

I now have the mere job of finishing this story. What in the good God's world is the use of anything? What, I ask you? Why am I writing to you? Why do you write to me? We are two howling maniacs in a single cell, trying to tear each other to pieces. Each suspects the other of the most horrible crimes. Each examines each word of the other's under a lens, looking, looking, looking for the worst possible construction. We ought never to write a word to each other. We ought never to speak. I ought to take what you give me in silence, and you ought to take what I give you in silence, and spit our galls out in the privacy of our cans until someday, mercifully, we both drop dead and end the agony.

I don't know when the novel will be finished. I really don't. I am going ahead with it on the same night-and-day schedule, but it's going to be even tougher now, when I have the absolute knowledge that no matter how it turns out, once again I have scored a goose egg. Only this time that pleasure has been moved up. I used to get it after I finished my part of the work. Now it's begun while the work is still in process. Well, that's one crime I can only charge myself with. I asked for it.

    MANNY

Tuesday morning [c. November 1948]

Dear Man:

    Yesterday I left the house early and did not return until late in the afternoon—to find your letter waiting for me. But I spent all day yesterday in two doctors' office, and came home so exhausted that I could not even open the mail.

    This will be a strange reply to your letter, so I had better give you this background. I don't think I have written anything to you about my physical ills this past year and a half, except in a general way. Well, here are the gruesome details—so that you will understand the strange nature of this reply to your letter.

    About six years ago I began having a pain in the lower right quadrant of my abdomen. In the past six years I have been examined by I-don't-know-how-many-doctors. The sum total of x-rays and God-knows-what was that no one ever knew the answer to my simple query: What causes the pain? Not one doctor ever doubted the existence of the pain—they all agreed it was there, that it wasn't imaginary.

    As perhaps you know, I simply got used to being in pain. Two summers ago—just after Bill and I got married—I got a particularly bad attack, lasting almost a month. Bill took me to a big doctor she knows, and for the first time I got an answer to my question. The doctor told me I had a spastic colon, which kicked up every once in a while. [. . .]

    This past summer my attacks were not as violent, but they sustained throughout most of the summer. I determined, however, since nerves are a heavily contributing cause, not to keep running to the doctor [...and...] when summer was over, I went in for a general check-up. The doctor found my chronic colitis still chronic, but something new turned up. This was not exactly a surprise. In view of my background and the history of my father and grandfather, I have been rather expecting it for a long time.

    In the course of a routine check-up of my kidneys, the doctor found that, in the medical phrase, I was "spilling" sugar. Followed quick blood tests and whatnot, with the result that I was told I had diabetes in a mild form. Not enough to require insulin at this time. But I was put on a diet, deprived of virtually every food I really like to eat, and told to lose weight, which I am doing very slowly.

    When the diabetes scare was over, I got my latest affliction. My mouth broke out with some sort of sores—on the inside of my cheeks, and on the lip. The worst thing about this is that it had the symptoms, superficially, of cancer.

Well, the rounds began again. I have seen four doctors (two yesterday) and so far can lay claim to four different diagnoses. It's amazing how I pick up obscure and controversial ailments.

The first diagnosis: that the infection was caused by my teeth. So I have had a complete (and expensive) overhauling of my teeth, including a new dental plate. Result: No visible improvement.

Second diagnosis: caused by a vitamin deficiency. So, for the last two weeks, I have been taking huge doses of vitamins. Result: No visible improvement, but—the highpowered vitamin consumption gave me vertigo and light-headedness. I have had the shakes now for two weeks, as if I were shell-shocked—that, it seems, is sometimes the effect caused by large vitamin doses.

Third diagnosis: caused by a fungus. So, I have been having, and am still having, treatments. So far, no improvement.

Fourth diagnosis: caused by excessive smoking. So, I was told to quit smoking immediately, and I haven't smoked in two weeks. Result: a different kind of shakes added to my other jitters.

While the doctors either did not know or did not agree on the cause, they did agree on two things: that the ailment was not cancer, and that I must not smoke again.

The upshot of all this is that I am absolutely pooped. With the worst fear eliminated, I think I will begin to recuperate more quickly now. I am so physically and mentally exhausted that I intend to take it easy for a few days and try to regain some strength.

So, when I staggered home yesterday and found your long letter, I simply did not have the strength, Man, to read it. Nor did I think it fair to either of us for me to read whatever you wrote in my present exhausted state. I have told you all this just so that you won't misunderstand my motives in not reading the letter.

Please give me a day or two to get back on my feet; then I will read the letter and write to you about it.

But as I sit in front of the typewriter this morning, I feel extraordinarily calm; and in this calmness I see clearly—without having read your letter—that surely the answer is very simple: I must have misunderstood you, and you must have misunderstood me, and we both keep misunderstanding each other—and probably will keep right on. And perhaps that really isn't too bad a thing, wearing as it is on our nerves and lives; it keeps both of us doing the best we possibly can, and while we are eternally suspicious of each other, and eternally hypersensitive to each other, the resultant work—coming out the hard way—is, strangely enough, the better for it. Sure, the price is high—and in that respect we both have simply got to learn to trust each other more.

Man, I'd appreciate a note from you in answer to this letter—just to tell me that you do understand my inability to read your letter now and to tackle any sort of reply to it.

As I sit here and review the past year and a half, I wonder at all that I have gone through: marriage and its unavoidable adjustments; finding a new home and building a new home life for the boys; the economic collapse; the ordeal of Steve's birth; and extraordinary expenses coming at a bad time; the unremitting ailments with which I have been afflicted.

All that and more. And yet, somehow, it had been an extraordinarily productive year. How I was able to accomplish so much work in this past year and a half, I just don't know. But I am definitely pooped now, and simply must regenerate.

With all my troubles and illnesses, I have been very happy with Bill. Perhaps that is the secret. I don't have to tell you that Bill is simply wonderful—and she has had immense adjustments to make herself. But she understands my physical and psychological problems, and helps me constantly to overcome them. [. . .]

I started out by saying this would be a strange reply to your letter, and it is. But I did not want you to misunderstand. In a couple of days I'll feel better, and then I shall do my damnedest, Man, to read and answer your letter without an iota of suspicion in me, and in a spirit of mutual understanding.

P.S. I should have told you this: during the last week, when I was both scared and ill, I simply had to run away somehow. So I finished up the first draft of the outline of a new novel—it got my mind off my troubles, and it got down on paper what was still fermenting in my brain. I have put the draft away, and I'll go back to it in a week or two. It would be dangerous, on second thought, to delay finishing it, and sending it on to you. In the past, when something has been put aside, it has remained aside permanently. We simply cannot afford to let this happen now. God knows what you will think of the new novel; God knows what I think of it; we shall see.

DAN

Friday Nov. 12 [1948].

Dear Dan:

I read your letter with considerable shock, but that, I think, was more because of the cumulative effect of all your ills than any real surprise. Certainly, as I seem to recall at least once before in the past, it would have been far better for both of us in our interrelationship if you had informed me before of all that you've been going through physically. It would have enabled me to understand what has not been very clear and, to that extent, it would have made my own reactions more balanced. This in turn would have reduced points of irritation on your part.

I am very interested.

Judging by the past, I'm inclined to think that what I have to say will not meet with a sympathetic reception from you; but I urge you to give some credence to my advice. [. . .]

I think the answer to your physical ills lies in the realm of psychosomatic medicine. It's only relatively recently that doctors found out that just as bodily ailments might cause emotional disturbances, so emotional disturbances might cause bodily ailments. It's often reciprocal.

From the little I know about it through reading, there seem to be certain bodily ailments in which emotional factors play an important, often a determining part. The ailments are real, not imaginary.

One of these ailments is diabetes.

Another is eczema—skin eruptions of various types.

Another is asthma.

Another is heart disease.

Another is hypertension. And so on. [. . .]

In relation to sufferers from heart ailments, still psychosomatically speaking, it has been found that such people characteristically are "hard workers, driving themselves without mercy and apparently enjoying it." They are "proud of the long hours they work, and incidentally resentful of the little appreciation they get for it . . ." "These patients were remarkable in the apparent strength but actual extreme brittleness of their defenses. They were strong only as long as a highly unified, highly crystallized life role turned out to be something to which they were culturally well adapted and which they found rewarding. But their brittle shell covered a mental poverty or an insecurity which had no other defenses once the shell was cracked. It seemed to make little difference whether the shell was broken from without or within. The result was rapid transition to bodily ailment. Just as the hard work is less responsible than the emotional conditions which led to it, so the heart-disease patient's characteristic carelessness of health, irregular eating habits, frequent excessive use of tobacco and coffee, disregard of sleep and so on are danger signals. They are not necessarily dangers. *In some cases, the abandonment of these bad habits is likely to set up a new emotional disturbance even worse than the one replaced...*Before it is safe for them to give up the bad habits they already have, they must be helped to understand why they have them. Otherwise, they will perhaps fly to even worse habits and an even more difficult disease. Usually they respond to treatment rather more readily than the fracture patient. That is because they have had long practice of working things out for themselves, instead of leaving them to others, and so they begin to work out their own cases. Generally they have done a great deal of thinking, even as children. Throughout life their physical reaction to an emotional problem was far more likely to be in words than in impulsive action. They will brood over their illness in solitude instead of talking it over."

In regard to diabetics, psychosomatically speaking still: "Emotional stability will cut down the physical reactions to the disease—the fatigue, the debility, the loose co-ordination, the irritability . . . The first great difficulty in helping diabetics achieve this stability is their reluctance to discuss their real emotions . . . They have a tendency to deny the existence of any conflicts at all."

* * *

[. . .] I know that I'm hardly the "shining example" of the advice-giver. On the other hand, I haven't been troubled by actual somatic manifestations as you have been. Your ailments are and have been causing you pain, suffering, anxiety—not to mention money!—some or most of which might be avoided by co-operation with the properly qualified physician. The psychosomatic technique is fairly recent and many doctors in physiological fields are either ignorant of it or untrained in it.

The therapeutic answer for you may well lie in placing yourself in the hands of a physician qualified to interpret physical symptoms in terms of emotional ills. That you have deeply underlying emotional disturbances, as I have, I don't think you can or would deny. That you don't know their real nature, any more than I do mine, is also obvious. What you need is to gain experience of your own emotions and conflicts and of their influence on your body. You can only get that experience through consultation with someone qualified by training and ability in this highly specialized field.

Why don't I follow my own advice? As I said, or implied, I suppose I have the typical resistance of our kind and so far nothing has happened to my body to compel me to seek assistance.

* * *

About us.

You don't have to bother writing a reply to my volume. The hell with it. You have other things to do, and so have I. The best thing is to file-and-forget.

On the novel: I am still crawling on my hands and knees and the Nov. 15 date is now unattainable. [. . .]

I have had the greatest difficulty maintaining a respectable pace in writing the novel. Every sentence is wrung out. Why this should be I swear I don't know, as it reads awfully smoothly and well. But there are no "soft spots" in it that race on the machine. It's my first such experience with a Queen novel.

Let me plug along at it. I'm worried enough about the unconscionable amount of time it's taking without having to smother my guilt feelings about it, too. It isn't from lack of effort or time, God knows. It's just a dog for pace. I have found myself trying to cut corners and race it and the only result has been wasted effort and, in sum, a slowing down. It doesn't work. Undoubtedly, emotional factors are present, and our relationship hasn't helped.

As for what you are or have been doing, take it easy. I know your compulsions, since I know mine. I think we each of us know that the other fellow isn't lazing around leading the life of Riley. Some things just can't be speeded up, and some circumstances just can't be ignored.

* * *

There is one thing you wrote in your letter that pleased and relieved me enormously. That was about your relationship with Bill. I had been getting the feeling, over months of correspondence in which you scarcely mentioned Bill's name, that things between you hadn't been going too well. What you wrote was a vast and agreeable denial of that theory and I am very glad, for both your sakes. I think Bill is swell and there's no question that she's had a tough row to hoe. She deserves the best—and I don't mean financially—and if you remain aware of her position and her personal problems, whatever they may be, you can't fail, with your start, to make a successful marriage. Kaye and I have struggled along for over six years under many handicaps and I think the only thing that has kept us together has been a basic willingness and eagerness on both our parts to solve our common problems; without that, we would have fallen by the wayside long ago.

* * *

[. . .] Regards to the family—and consider what I wrote you!

MANNY

Monday Nov 29, 1948

Dear Dan:

[. . .] About the novel: to date, about 350 pages of the manuscript are in *finished* form—that is, ready to be shipped. I have worked this one a little differently from previous jobs for a number of reasons. I estimate that there will probably be closer to 400 pages in the complete job. [. . .]

I suggest you don't get a conniption or start burning the U.S. mails over any of this. Where this book is concerned, my conscience is as clear as a California sky in June. I've worked harder and more consistently on this one than on anything in the past. It is just a slave-driving dog. I bogged down two weeks ago from sheer auto-intoxication. Ten days passed without more than about 5 pages of script done. I have been at this so damned long I'd got to the point of nerve-and-will exhaustion. Nothing I wrote was right during that period. I threw away a ream of paper. It was in a particularly tough part of the book and I collapsed on myself at the crucial time. Besides, I've had to do a lot of research. I'm dealing with actualities—it's not like writing about Wrightsville, which was cut out of the whole cloth. Even physically the job is big. Making an original and four carbons for every page in itself takes a lot of time. [. . .] The results, despite the delays, are going to be gratifying—always, I hasten to add, in my opinion. I can't begin to say what you will think of it. But I am convinced that this will be considered, from every standpoint—both plot and writing—the very finest Queen novel to date, by just about a million miles. I think it has a good chance of being considered a sort of classic, at least among the cognoscenti. I have neither highbrowed it not looked down on it. I have been, and am, looking at it as a serious jog, very serious indeed. I think it will be a cinch for the movies. I even think we may find ourselves in the enviable position of getting competitive bids on it. This is one job I'd like to see peddled to the movies from galley.

What I have ahead of me now is the home stretch, which is going to be relatively easy. I'm in sight of the tape and running strongly. Two weeks should finish it up. What I am going to do is send you the whole thing—all four of the outside copies, including the original—if you'd like. Or would you prefer to have me send you your copy and hold back the others till I hear from you? I would like you to read the manuscript in the original, rather than in a lousy carbon. Let me know.

I don't know yet how I came to underestimate the extent and ramifications of this job. Looking back on it now, I'm amazed at my lack of foresight.

Just keep your shirt on and wait. It won't be long now.

Our love to Bill and the kids–

MANNY

1949: 'This Negro Business'

Lee's belief in *Cat of Many Tails* was fully justified. He thought it might be "considered a sort of classic". He was right. *Cat* is considered by many critics to be the apogee of Queen's art. With good reason: *Cat* offers myriad delights. It possesses the psychological complexity of *Wonder*, presents a vivid portrait of post-war Manhattan, and infuses moral and intellectual content into an incredibly suspenseful story of pursuit. A difficult challenge, neatly pulled off. If Jimmy and Celeste don't move beyond their Hollywood-love-interest origins, they don't really hurt the book; they're a minor flaw in a major work.

There was to be no magazine or movie sale for *Cat*. A television movie version entitled *Ellery Queen: Don't Look Behind You* appeared in 1971 on NBC to no acclaim whatsoever. Co-writers Richard Levinson and William Link were so dismayed with what had been done to their script that they had their names removed from the credits and replaced with a pseudonym. Four years later, Levinson and Link would successfully bring EQ to the small screen.

Dannay and Lee disagreed so frequently on practically everything that it is a surprise to discover their mutual distaste for the abridged version of Raymond

Chandler's *The Little Sister*, first published in the April 1949 issue of *Cosmopolitan*. A craftsman's disdain and a strain of prudery are evident in Lee's response. In Dannay's, envy—and dismay: Why should *Sister* be published and *Cat* left yowling for a home?

Two other issues—one relatively small, one much larger—are the subjects of much discussion in these letters from 1949. The first is the question of a title for the novel that was published as *Cat of Many Tails*. Dannay and Lee often had to hunt for the right title, a common problem. The larger issue also involves *Cat* and has to do with what Lee calls "this Negro business." Both cousins were good liberals, committed to freedom of speech and equal rights. How the element of race manifests itself in *Cat* also reflects the ways in which Dannay and Lee attempted to navigate shifting commercial and aesthetic demands while keeping their work in touch with the times.

Fascinating, too, is Dannay's description of Ellery Queen's Jewish identity. Daniel Nathan (Dannay) and Emanuel Lepofsky (Lee) were acutely aware of their Jewish heritage. Anyone who has read the books knows that Ellery's sense of ethics, his love of justice, of books and learning is quintessentially Jewish.

Cat of Many Tails is a riveting story with all the Queenian hallmarks, but its intricately detailed portrait of the City lifts it into another category entirely; you would swear you were in Manhattan in the late '40s. An even more striking aspect of the novel concerns Ellery's malaise and the way he transcends the personal and professional crises stemming from the events of *Ten Days' Wonder*.

The "world theme" also provides the book with yet another layer of complexity: the city's panic reflects that of the post-War world. Rich with atmosphere and ideas, *Cat* is a masterful work of fiction.

The "Edith" mentioned below is Edith Haggard, Dannay and Lee's literary agent at the Curtis Brown Agency. "Ommerle" is Harry Ommerle, an agent for William Morris.

April 12, 1949

Dear Man:

[. . .] I still am not smoking—nearly six months now—and if possible I'm going to give up smoking altogether; the infection in my mouth which necessitated giving up smoking is much improved, but not entirely gone; on the other hand, no-smoking has definitely helped my colonic condition and stomach trouble—I am not nearly as distressed as I used to be. But there are days when I still get attacks, and I am miserable for the duration of the distress. [. . .]

I have heard nothing from Little, Brown—no reaction at all. Edith is still working on a possible magazine shot. *[The Saturday Evening Post]* turned it down pronto—merely said it was too much of a whodunit, with not enough "romance". [. . .]

While I think of it: I wish you would read the Raymond Chandler "complete novel" in the current *Cosmopolitan*. Let me know your reaction. I am seriously thinking of stepping out of the editor's shoes and writing a review of this "book"—blasting it as one of the most shameful pieces of magazine publication I have ever read—bought and published wholly because of Chandler's name. The story struck me as incredibly cheap, crude, with all the worst faults of hardboiledism, and from the apparently unimportant viewpoint of simple clarity, I do not know what the hell the story is about, who killed who, or why, or how, or where—or anything. And where in this story is "what magazines want"?

No, the hell with it. It is better for Queen not to be a critic that way. But I would like to know your opinion of the story. By the way, too: The cat story is now at *Cosmopolitan*—in fact, has been there about two weeks. If *Cosmo* bought the Chandler piece, I don't see how they can even think of turning down the cat story! That Chandler story actually encouraged me: I think we'll sell to *Cosmo*! I am dead serious. [. . .]

Now I'm working on another basic idea. I don't know if this one will work out either, but I like it and am pushing ahead. The interesting thing about this new theme is that I already have the perfect, the inevitable title for the book!

Two titles ahead—but still no really good title for the Cat.

Which, roundabout, gets me to the magazine. True, I worked ahead to give me time for the new novel, but I should tell you that there is no such thing any more as working ahead on the magazine and having free time. Despite my working ahead, the magazine intrudes every day. The magazine, Man, grows to bigger and bigger demands on my time—and it's got me worried. I no longer can really get away from it, and have really uninterrupted time for other work. There are many reasons. Two of them are: it is getting harder and harder to find good *new* material—the boys and girls are not writing fine stuff in the short form. The annual contest saves our skins every year now, so far as new stories are concerned; but the annual contest is also a tremendous headache and a hell of a lot of work. Second reason: it is getting harder and harder to find good *old* material—hence, my sudden request for fill-ins on the O'Brien and O. Henry volumes.

Listen to this: not only is it hard to find good old stories, but it is getting harder and harder to *clear the rights*. Get this: of the last 35 requests to buy reprint rights for *EQMM*, we were turned down on *20*!!! Whether this is a bad period or an actual trend, I don't know. Agents and authors are saying no more often than they did—though the Lord only knows why in these admittedly tough (and getting tougher) times. [. . .]

The one bright spot has been the magazine—hence, my deep-rooted conviction that I must do all I can to keep the magazine going at the top of its form (which includes my "peculiar" editorial comments). Result: I have less time than I hoped to work on a new novel, and as a further consequence, it goes slowly—very slowly. And I am tired. After all, Man, my output these last two years has really been too much to expect: the novels alone would be a healthy output; the editing of the magazine alone would be a full-time job; to say nothing of all the incidentals and lost time.

It's a gloomy picture. Speaking for myself, I need a "break" desperately. A magazine sale or a radio sale would give me a much needed—desperately needed—lift. Not only financially—but perhaps even more important, in morale. Some kind of break would remove from my mind the growing conviction that the general collapse we have had—hell, you know what I mean. Where is rock-bottom?

All of this has made me mighty tough to live with. Hilda gets the dirty end of it.

Perhaps I shouldn't write—maybe it would be better that way.

DAN

April 14, 1949

Dear Man:

Last night I went to Hilda's mother's house for the first Passover Seder—and came away with a possible title for the cat story.

The prayer-book of the Passover holiday is, as you know, The Haggadah of Passover—the word Haggadah means "a telling," or the "narrative" or "story." Now, one of the traditional Passover songs is, as you probably remember, "Chad Gadya."

In Chad Gadya is the following:

And The Cat Came

This strikes me as an excellent title for the book—or, rather, I should say that the more I think of it, the more I like it. It is simple, yet unusual; it has, for all its simplicity, a definite flavor; and it seems to me to be terribly ominous.

If used, I would suggest a fuller quotation, on the half-title page of the dedication, together with the source—as follows:

And the cat came and ate the kid. . .

Chad Gadya, Haggadah

Jewish people, of course, would recognize the source as part of the Passover service; but Gentiles would probably ascribe the quotation to ancient Aramaic or Sanskrit, or something—which is perfectly all right. Either way, the quotation and source sound *important*. The Chad Gadya has many meanings, as a parable. The song is an ancient version of "The House That Jack Built," with the various animals and objects representing, allegorically, the persecutors of the Jews. For example, the Assyrian *cat*, the Babylonian *dog*, the Persian *fire*, the Roman *waters*, etc. The "kid" (baby goat) represents the Jew—oppressed, persecuted, burned, drowned, etc.—but never eliminated. The persecutors die out, the "kid" (Jew) survives.

Of course, there is a deep symbolical meaning here. True, it has only a far-fetched connection symbolically with the novel itself, but the symbolism appeals to me nevertheless. After all, even though we would be subtle about it, the authors of the book are Jews, and in all the deepest senses, so is Ellery Queen the character. [. . .]

By the way, too: A title starting with *And* has the practical advantage of placing the book at the head, or near the head, of any list of books arranged alphabetically.

What do you think?

* * *

[. . .] Herbert Mayes, now editor of both *Good Housekeeping* and *Cosmopolitan*, has turned down the novel. No comment other than—not suitable for *G.H.* and apparently equally unsuitable for *Cosmo*.

I don't think I ever felt so low in morale about the magazine situation. *Please* read the Raymond Chandler story in the current issue of *Cosmo* and tell me how in the name of all that's reasonable, Mayes could buy the Chandler shit and reject the cat story? How? How? [. . .]

DAN

Saturday April 16 [1949]

Dear Dan:

[. . .] Against my best judgment I went out and bought *Cosmo*. Why you inflicted this on me I don't understand, unless it's because you have a sadistic desire to punish me for some unnamed crime. I've wasted thirty-five good cents and a couple of hours of time that well could have been spent otherwise. All right, it's crud, so what? Crud is what they want. Crud is what they'll always want. This one has the merit of having several different shades and sizes of crud—it has tits in it, a nipple that's as hard as a ruby, "mammaries," and at least three mentions of "sleeping with you." And a French kiss with the hero's tongue being half bitten off. It also has a number of corpses, a lot of blood, and two hours' worth of absolute, dead-center boredom. [. . .] It is not merely crud—it is plain shit. Oh—and yes, it makes no sense. None at all. I didn't understand it when I read it and I don't understand it now [. . .] I don't even know which character is which and—secret—I don't even give a good goddamn. I didn't even while reading.

I tell you it's a good thing Mayes didn't take the Queen story. It's healthy. It proves that what we have to offer is sane, clean, understandable, and entertaining. Because obviously what he wants is something crazy, filthy, incomprehensible, and dull. And *you* were the one who accused me of writing *indirectly*!

Forget it. Forget the whole stinking bunch of highbinding fakers. The writers are fakers and the editors are fakers and God knows the readers are fakers if they "like" the shit the writer-editor-fakers give them. They *can't* like it. It's not possible. I doubt if even Mayes likes it. Certainly Chandler doesn't. It's just that he found the magic shit-formula of crap-tit-cryptic-utterance that makes men like Mayes say, "Ah, the Hemingway of the slick field!" [. . .]

* * *

[*The Saturday Evening Post*] says the story hasn't "enough romance." Romance is one thing to [*The Saturday Evening Post*] and another to *Cosmo* and *Good Housekeeping*. [. . .] Also, the surface has to be "slick." They mean by "slick" the hard, millicron-thick veneer of sophistication-leer-tongue-in-cheek-we're-hep-boys-worldly-wise-night-club-stripper-rod-"quietly"-obscure-dialogue-reeferaddictswhoreshomosmobsters and, of course, the "hero" who hasn't a moral scruple in his makeup, gets a hardon at the sight of every beautiful dame, lays her within thirty minutes of meeting her, hits her in the jaw with his gun, stops a bullet or a knife in every chapter, knows from nothing all through—"it's a mystery, see?"—then at the end "All of a sudden it figures—it adds up, chum"—and he adds it up for us in wild arithmetic not even a maniac could make sense of. Oh, yes, and one mustn't forget that the hero is always at odds with the regular police; they suspect him, they don't like him, they pull him in, they curse him, at the end they listen to him and grab off the credit.

The above is the formula. Do a plot like that about people like that and write it in words of not more than two syllables with lots of cryptic dialogue, nothing ever quite making sense—and, I almost forgot—at least once have your detective quote poetry, just to show he got past the fourth grade in his youth—and hell, you've got a serial sale to *Cosmo*. Maybe it requires a bit more finesse for [*The Saturday Evening Post*]—about *them* I wouldn't know.

What are you beating your brains out for? Why worry? Is it the money? There are lots of guys making a good living out of robbing banks, does that mean you have to rob banks, too? Recognize the facts. They want shit, they are shit, and it takes a shit expert to satisfy them. Unfortunately, neither of us quite qualifies. We'll just have to struggle along the hard way.

* * *

[. . .] About your title suggestion, *And The Cat Came*. I've deliberately not responded (it is now Sunday) for a couple of days, mulling it over in my mind, trying to get used to it, making more than the usual effort since it's obvious you like it very much. I could live with it, it wouldn't bother me, I might even get to like it after a fashion, but I still have the feeling it isn't "right." After all, the title has to stand on its own feet, regardless of source, as you say yourself.

I've been trying to analyze what it is about it that bothers me. I think again it's its very literary flavor. I've always been bothered by titles starting with "And." The "And" seems so unnecessary, so out of tune with modernity—so Biblical. And this is a modern story in every sense.

Maybe I'm way off on this. Maybe you're right. I don't know. [. . .]

I don't want to seem arbitrary about *And The Cat Came*, because I don't feel that way. It's a definite possibility. But I just can't be enthusiastic about it. Let's wait a while longer. Maybe [Little, Brown editor Stanley] Salmen will come up with something. Meanwhile, we can be mulling some more.

[. . .] It is now Monday afternoon, April 18. I've had a severe bout of sinus which has been taking my head off by the roots, on top of a cold which has now lasted two weeks without signs of giving up, But I won't make the mistake of boring you with my physical ailments—I mean the same mistake. Mine seem to be trifling compared with yours. Although, of course, not to me. (It's all in whose ass is being kicked, I guess.) [. . .]

Your low spirits find an echo in mine, of course. Everything seems to have collapsed at the same time. The most serious is of course the reprint situation. I frankly don't understand it. I agree that something has to happen quickly or 1949 will be a year of decision. If Ommerle can't come up with at least a summer replacement [time slot for the Ellery Queen radio show], the only source of outside income with a reasonable percentage of probability or at least possibility, I don't see how either of us is to make the faintest stab at getting along this year.

Obviously, the magazine must be maintained as the backbone of running income. If you find it difficult or next to impossible to run the magazine and go ahead on a new novel as well, I see no alternatives but this: Either for you to get some help on the magazine work which will substantially reduce your load (which you have said in the past was impracticable) or for me to try to take up on the novel where you've left off and get the whole thing out from that point on, leaving you with nothing to worry about but the magazine. [. . .] Tell me in which way you think I can be of the fullest service, taking into consideration only your own feelings and ailments and incapacities of the moment. [. . .] For myself, I am excluding all consideration of my own preferences in action. It would be helpful, I think, if you did the same and discussed this with me purely from the point of what has to be done.

The weather has been stinking here this month. And I don't imagine I've been any easier to live with than you have.

Regards to Hilda and the boys.

MANNY

Raymond Chandler (1888–1959) famously—and waspishly—refused to take part in a "Who Are the 10 Best Living Mystery Writers?" poll which Fred Dannay conducted for *Ellery Queen's Mystery Magazine* in the early 1950s. He is, of course, one of the greats himself, although *The Little Sister* is generally thought of as one of his lesser works...but not necessarily for the reasons given by Lee. It's a tired and cynical book. Chandler's disgust with Los Angeles, with the film industry, with himself and his circumstances, is palpable. Ironically, Chandler was also disgusted with the abridgment of *The Little Sister* that so offended Dannay and Lee. He disapproved of the way the novel was condensed, and of the various deletions and additions *Cosmopolitan* made along the way. The only nice thing about the whole affair was the money—Chandler received $10,000. One sees why Dannay so desperately wished for a magazine sale.

The vulgarity and violence Lee condemns in Chandler is perhaps a more fitting response to Mickey Spillane's work, which was setting post-war records in paperback sales and titillation. Spillane has his advocates, but Dannay and Lee were not among them, and the ultra-hardboiled detective who thinks with his fists was parodied in a number of their books and stories, and on the EQ radio show.

Lee's dislike for titles beginning with 'And' evidently withered over the years: *And On The Eighth Day* (1964) is one of the most striking and original of the later EQ novels. (Ghostwritten, yes, but that doesn't detract from its strengths.)

April—who knows? [1949]

Dear Man,

[. . .] I do *not* want to work exclusively on the magazine. It is not my wish, either consciously or subconsciously. It has never even occurred to me—and I say that most positively. In fact, I would fight against any such arrangement of work. For one thing, I do not want to give up creative work entirely; much as I detest the drain and heartache and brainache of creative work, I could not even bring myself to give it up. For another thing, the magazine does not require full-time work—at least, it does not require it from me now. True, the magazine work grows steadily—but it is not yet full-time. [. . .]

Your suggestion that you take up on the novel where I've left off and your getting the whole thing out from that point on—that suggestion, I must confess, scared the shit out of me. I wonder if you realize what this means—to both of us. From the standpoint of time alone, I seriously question if any time would be saved by this method. Surely you realize you spent nine months on the cat story—after the plot was completely finished. Do you realize how much time might be required to take up on the new novel from whatever point I left off? [. . .]

Think of the basic disagreements through which we suffer now—with the work supposedly demarcated along definitely agreed lines. Never once, Man, despite all your promises to accept my end of the job, have you ever really accepted my work. How could your suggestion lead to anything but infinitely more grief?

Of course, I must admit that I do not even understand the motive behind your suggestion. Is this what you *want* to do? Is it that psychologically you really want me to become tied up exclusively with the magazine, that deep down you really want me to give up my end of the novels? I don't know, and I won't even try to guess. I'm just stumped.

* * *

[. . .] I still like *And The Cat Came*—but suppose we continue brooding about it. Something else may crop up. How do you like this?—*Mr. Cat.* I see that the new Bing Crosby picture is going to be called *Mr. Music. Mr. Cat* does imply the King of Cats. Just a thought . . .

* * *

[. . .] I have had no word from Salmen regarding his reaction to the novel. Edith Haggard phoned me today—to tell me that you had written to her and that she had replied; she told me that she had forgotten to tell me any of the specific [*Good Housekeeping*] and *Cosmo* reactions, and reminded herself when she wrote them to you—so you knew these facts even before I did.

I tell you what I know. I can't tell you what I don't know myself.

* * *

Another day gone . . .

DAN

Saturday Apr. 23 [1949]

Dear Dan:

[. . .] Let us understand each other once and for all on this matter. I don't want to encroach on your prerogatives. I don't want to do the plotting. I dislike plotting. What's more, I don't do it as well as you do. Keep the plotting. PLEASE. But for Christ's sake, don't keep telling me how tough it is if you don't want and won't accept any offer on my part to take it over—offers made *as a result, and only as a result,* of your complaints. I'm relieved that you want to hold on to the novel-plotting. I'm even grateful to you. But I don't like putting out my hand when I think you need it—as a result of your own actions— and having you examine it for a hidden dagger. I don't think you'd like it, either. I know damned well you wouldn't.

Danny, what is your beef? What's eating you? Your letters are poisonous. You keep dropping little atom bombs under me. Why? Do you realize how suspicious you are? How you always assume there is a "hidden motive" in everything I say? How goddam touchy you are in everything? What nasty slaps you throw my way at every conceivable opportunity? This business of Edith Haggard, for instance, with which you end your letter—just symptomatic. You wrote me what she had told you. You said yourself "that was all she said," or words to that effect. I wanted to find out more. I wrote to her. She replied. I promptly wrote to you telling you what she wrote to me. I wound up by saying that either you misunderstood her or she told you something quite different— there were no other possibilities, as what you wrote me she said and what she wrote to me were simply not of a piece. I was not criticizing or accusing you of anything. I was criticizing her. Yet you write me curtly: "I tell you what I know. I can't tell you what I don't know myself," as if I had accused you of withholding or falsifying information. Certainly you tell me what you know. Certainly you can't tell me what you don't know yourself. Who said you don't? Who said you could? Who even inferred it? Why snap back? Why the hell write at all, in fact?

* * *

[. . .] *Mr. Cat* grows on me. Let it gestate a while

Tony has been laid up for an entire week with a temperature that seems to be flu, he is currently taking radium treatments for his nose, the baby has just come down with a temperature, there is chicken pox across the street and may develop here as the children played with the infected child–

Sorry. Tony just threw up for the second time today and his temperature is close to 103. Looks as if he's popping something—chicken pox or measles— and we can't get our fancy Beverly Hills pediatrician to make the trip out here, so the hell with him—we're calling in a local man—and it looks like a siege.

Be seeing you.

MANNY

The creative and personal differences between Dannay and Lee are illustrated sharply and at length when the question of race enters the picture.

Race is an element of *Cat of Many Tails*, as it is a part of New York City, the book's setting (and major character, along with Ellery himself). How race is utilized, though, is the bone of contention between the cousins, and its artistic and social ramifications are hotly disputed. Both of them want to be just and fair and impartial, and believe the other has failed in that task. In actuality, they are passionate men of liberal belief who are fighting on the side of the angels.

Little, Brown editor Stanley Salmen asked Dannay if Lee would make a number of cuts in the *Cat* manuscript. Lee refused; he believed the cuts were unnecessary and harmful. Hence the following letter from Dannay…

May 5, 1949

Dear Man:

You say that you are *convinced* that your decision not to make the cuts is absolutely right, that to make the cuts would damage the book; you say that your conviction is not emotional bias, that it is an intellectual conviction; you say that your conviction has nothing to do with principle of prerogatives, that it is purely and simply your feeling of rightness for the book itself.

Manny, has it ever once occurred to you that I too can feel exactly this way? That I too can have a purely intellectual conviction, that I too can be convinced, deeply, completely, that I know what is best for the work? Perhaps you have thought of it, but I am positive that you have never done more than merely acknowledge the possible existence in me of such deep and positive convictions.

For a long time, Man, I have had a growing feeling that you limit my range of convictions. I don't doubt that you credit me with a certain creative ingenuity, what you call a "peculiar" talent; but when it comes to deeper critical convictions, to larger literary and creative knowledge and feelings, I'm afraid you rank me rather low. I have a certain brilliance in plot construction and conception, but I have the feeling you consider all this a rather superficial accomplishment—that when it comes to the more important varieties and philosophies of writing, I am just a clever contriver.

Our work is supposedly so clearly demarcated that I simply have stuck, as much as I can, to my end of the job. That is why I have never done anything but make suggestions about the writing. That is your province, and I have done my best to let you be the final authority in your province. That is why I have deeply resented your unwillingness to let me be the final authority in my province. When I want the plot a certain way, and you change it, and I disagree most strongly, and you refuse to do it my way, you are exercising the final authority not only in your end of the work, but in mine. That you are wrong in this— utterly and unfairly wrong—is my deepest conviction; if you are the final authority in the writing, then you should acknowledge my final authority in the plotting. If you can have convictions about your end of the work, you should acknowledge my right to convictions about my end of the work.

Take your attitude to the magazine version. You did it much against your judgment and wishes. When you were finished with the magazine version, you went on record as saying that it was utterly bad, that all the good values of the book version were completely eliminated, that the magazine version could not possibly sell. Well, maybe it won't sell; but the reactions so far have proved you wrong. With any normal break in times and in publishing conditions, we would have sold the cat story to a magazine without the slightest trouble—indeed, it may still sell.

Does all this make it easy for me to accept your convictions as to what is best for the book, and what is best for our interests?

And how about my own convictions? You made one change in the cat story that has spoiled this story for me for all time. You say that, as I know, you are very partial to this book, that you are proud of your part in it, and that all this makes it even harder for you to "submit to 'compromise'" when I am dead certain in my own mind that to excise the questionable material would be a loss—not to me—but to the book." [. . .]

Let me go into just one change you made in the book—the matter of the murder of the Negro girl. I made my position utterly clear. Let me repeat it, so that there won't be any misconception about it. I said that I was absolutely against a Negro murder for the magazines. This was purely and simply a matter of practicality. I felt that no magazine would print the Negro murder passage as you wrote it; nor did I think any magazine would buy the story with a Negro murder in it, even with the minimum of implications you insisted on.

That was the magazine end of it. You agreed to delete the Negro murder for magazines. You did not agree because you thought I was right; you agreed simply because you didn't think the story had any magazine chance anyway, and because you didn't give a damn about the magazine version.

For the book version, which was your only concern, I again made my position crystal clear. I said I was willing to have a Negro murder providing it was not the murder which brought Ellery actively into the case. I fought for this position passionately. I was willing to have a Negro murder before Ellery came into the case, or after, but I did not want a Negro murder to be the instrument which made Ellery come out of retirement.

Manny, we may both be on the same side of the fence, in our feelings toward the Negro question; but we certainly don't agree on how this feeling should be expressed. Every time I read a manuscript of the cat story, I writhed inside at the Negro passage; every time I think of that part of the story, I squirm inside.

It is terribly wrong, in my deepest possible conviction, to make Ellery come into the case the way he now does. The Negroes do not want special treatment; they want equal treatment. If Ellery could not bring himself to enter the case as the result of a series of white murders, he should not come in as the result of a Negro murder. That is a kind of nasty and evil tolerance which turns my insides; that is a kind of intellectualized tolerance that is, in my opinion, the worst type of intolerance. And I feel so strongly on this matter that for me the book was spoiled. After all, Man, the name Ellery Queen belongs to both of us; its use affects both of us personally. That book, signed Ellery Queen, stands for me too; what it says publicly reflects my thinking and feelings; and it says something I abhor deeply. In the same way, Ellery Queen the character stands for the two of us; what Ellery does as a character reflects the two of us personally; and what

Ellery does in this book is not me; his reaction to the Negro problem is not me; [. . .] what Ellery does in this book does not reflect me.

This book is lost for me, on that one count alone. I can never think of it, or look at it, with anything but shame inside. I don't say that you have a nasty and evil kind of tolerance; I think you have a genuine tolerance, but I think, most sincerely, that you expressed your tolerance in a deeply intolerant way.

This may give you some idea of how deep my convictions are. Yet, no matter how hard I fight with you to respect my convictions, in the end you do it your way. I even discussed all this with you face to face, rather than by phone or letter; and yet I lost. I not only lost, but you went back home after our face to face discussion, and not only vetoed my plea, but—do you realize it?—you added salt to my wound, you twisted the knife again. Why did you change the name Wilkins to White? Knowing how I felt about this murder as the Negro murder, how could you change the name of the Negro girl to White—thus artificially emphasizing the color significance?

I don't know what you will think of all this. You may even twist it into some theory that, deep down, I am really a bigot of the worst type. Whatever you finally think, so be it; I would never have written this except that you wrote me about your convictions, and how in the face of what others feel and think, you can still decide what *you* think is best for the book. Deep, deep down inside of me, with all the conviction that a human being can possibly have, I feel that Ellery did a shameful thing, an unforgivably intolerant thing, and for the rest of my life I will shun this book, and what it stands for, in my mind and heart.

You write of how you are partial to this book, how proud you are of your part in it, and how hard it is for you to compromise. Manny, this book was born in me; it grew inside of me; I nurtured it, created it. Yet in some of its most important aspects, I had nothing to say about it; you vetoed my convictions, ignored my pleas to keep the book what I originally conceived it. My partiality to the book, my pride, my deepest convictions gradually disintegrated; and now you ask me to accept, fully and wholeheartedly, your final fight to retain *your* convictions on what the book should be, and what is best for it. [. . .]

There is another factor which I think you ignore completely: you feel that without these long passages on the "world theme," the readers will not accept the panic of a whole city losing its head; you feel that you, in at least a couple of passages, must bring out the confusion and insecurity of the times, of 1949 specifically. Don't you think your readers feel this confusion and insecurity themselves? Don't you think today's readers, reading the cat story, *bring to it* the realization (whether they know the causes or not) of world-wide confusion and insecurity? You don't have to give the reader concentrated doses of this feeling; it is here; it is in all readers' consciousness, whether they are aware of it or not; it exists; and the events in the story will tie in, even subconsciously, with that prevalent mood which all people, of all stations, feel today. Don't you think the very existence of this 1949 temper had a great deal to do with my conceiving this story, and with my development of the basic theme? I couldn't have planned this story in 1938 or 1921; and the readers couldn't have appreciated this story in 1938 or 1921; but they can read it in 1949—without being hit over the head with the reminder that it is 1949; and they can accept the story because all around them it is 1949, because in their minds it is 1949, because they—the readers themselves—bring the "world theme" (however they may imagine it, or interpret it, in their own individual existences) to the book.

I have tried to write this letter as dispassionately, as reasonably, as intelligently, as understandingly, as I can. I would like to repeat your own final paragraph, and ask you to do the same—that is, in reading my letter, to remember that it is based on only one thing, to the best of my self-knowledge: A feeling of what's best for the book. I might go one step further than you did, and say that this letter is based on what's best not only for this book but for our collaborative work as a whole. For there is no possible question, Man, that our lack of mutual understanding, and our lack of delegated, final authority on our respective fields of effort, is hurting the work as a whole. [. . .]

Now I must get back to work. It will take me an hour to reorient myself to other problems. I only hope this letter proves helpful, not only to the specific problem but to the larger problems from which a single book stems.

DAN

I have characterized Dannay and Lee elsewhere in these pages as ambitious. How to achieve those ambitions, however, was a source of disagreement.

Dannay worked from inside the genre and spent his creative and editorial lives championing the mystery story's potential. Lee was less enamored of the form *per se*. *Cat of Many Tails'* "world theme" provides an illuminating look at what Lee considered "important" writing.

After a mass meeting erupts into violence, chaos sweeps the streets of Manhattan, with broken glass and looting and bloodshed following in its wake. Early the next morning, a battered Ellery sits in Rockefeller Center and dreams that the golden statue of mighty Prometheus speaks to him. What follows is a lengthy and overt rumination on the nature of humankind.

This section of the book is of philosophical interest, it provides perspective on the events of the book at a crucial point, and structurally it allows us a moment to catch our breath before we continue onward with the search for the Cat. Lee obviously liked it, too.

But Dannay did not. He believed that the age will speak for itself and that the reader, as a product of the age, will recognize the "confusions and insecurity of the times" without explicit prompting.

Whichever point of view one takes in the debate, there is no denying that the "world theme" section of *Cat* outlines as rigorous and bleak a view of the way things are as any hard-boiled novel.

May 9, 1949

Dear Dan:

[. . .] Now about this Negro business: Your discussion of this boils down to two things:

(1) I had no right to change one of your murders to a Negro murder; and (2) in placing it where I did I made Ellery do "a shameful thing, an unforgivably intolerant thing, and for the rest of my life I will shun this book, and what it stands for, in my mind and heart."

(1) Our controversy over our respective provinces in the collaboration is basic, chronic, and apparently hopeless of resolution. We agreed long ago to a division of the work: you to "do the plotting," I to "do the writing." But once that is said, we differ violently at every point. [. . .] The name Ellery Queen belongs to both of us and a book signed Ellery Queen stands for me too and what it says publicly reflects my thinking and feelings? You bet. Who has more control over what a book "says"—you or I? Every Queen book for God knows how many years now has "said" substantially what *you* wanted it to say—very substantially, I might add. The trouble with you is you want it to say *totally* what you want it to say. [. . .] The fact of the matter is that what Ellery has done and has been in any of the Queen books has largely reflected and been you. You have dictated his actions, you have dictated his psychology, his contacts, his cases, his solutions, his omissions as well as his commissions. You have no corner on the writhing market, Danny; I've writhed my full share. [. . .]

Danny, I have tried very hard not to step on your toes—harder than you'll ever know. In the past I have taken material legitimately and ineradicably part of the plot and made every effort to render it as your outline indicated, even when I disagreed violently with it. But this case presented a different situation. This was the first plot in which the identity of the victims in no way, shape or form affected the plot. The nine victims could have been anybody; in fact, that was the whole point. Nothing—I repeat, nothing—in the plot, in the events, the unfolding of the mystery part of the case would have been changed one particle; the solution would have remained identical. [. . .] What I'm trying to say is that in this one the very nature of your story seemed to give me more than the usual latitude with the characters without affecting the detective story one iota. Obviously, wholesale changes in characters would have made wholesale changes in material, but what material? That's exactly the point. To you *all* material is your sole domain; to me I have latitude in regard to material which does not affect the plot. It is true that this gives me some say in *story*; but how can anyone write a book, even from the most exhaustive plot outline, without exercising some influence on story? I maintain that I have a right to exercise some influence on story; I maintain that, whether I conceive myself as having the right or not, I can't *help* exercising some influence on story; no one could who had the job of writing from someone else's plot. Nor do you have the right to expect that I won't exercise some influence on story. [. . .]

The more I studied the outline the more I felt that some ingredient was missing. I knew it was in the characters. It was obvious that you had picked the characters to give a cross-section of New York, and with this conception I was in absolute and wholehearted agreement. Then I realized what wasn't there. In a realistic story of New York, in which the nine victims represented, or should have represented, "New York," one of the strongest minorities was not represented—one of the three great minorities which give New York its distinctive flavor, the Jews, the Irish, and the Negroes. The Jew and the Irishman were there, but no Negro. I didn't see how I could write a story about New York in which New York was a "character" without making one of the victims a Negro. To have *no* Negro would be nice-Nellyism, a sop to prejudice; he (or she) would stand out by his or her very absence—in this set-up particularly; the only possible justification for omitting a Negro would be not to step on anybody's "toes"—meaning on the toes of people who don't think Negroes and whites should mix on any level, even death; the people who practice segregation even in cemeteries. The whole conception of the story was too good to be spoiled by an omission which, on any realistic basis, it was necessary to include. It was inconceivable to me that your personal feelings, consciously or unconsciously, dictated the omission; I thought you just either hadn't thought of it or, if you had, you left it out without realizing the implications of your omission. Later it became clear that your chief reason either for not thinking of it or for rejecting it if you did think of it was that you felt any Negro murder in the series would militate against a magazine sale. It was easy for me to have overlooked this since this story never at any time seemed to me to be a magazine story. Nevertheless, when you pointed it out to me, agreed to omit the Negro murder entirely from the magazine version and change the character back to a white girl. [. . .] It's true I didn't think the story had a magazine chance, but it's a goddam untruth that that was the reason I agreed to the change for the magazine version; it's the snide kind of thing you're so fond of ascribing to me. It's also a very shortsighted distortion to say that I didn't give a damn about the magazine version. I worked my ass off on that version—and I'll tell you something else—it's damn snotty of you to charge me with not giving a damn about the magazine version when you know what work I put into that version. [. . .]

This brings me to:

(2) I not only made Beatrice Wilkins a Negro, but I placed her murder in the

spot "which brought Ellery actively into the case," which made a Negro murder
... "the instrument which made Ellery come out of retirement." In doing so, I
exhibited "a kind of nasty and evil tolerance which turns my insides. [. . .] I feel
so strongly on this matter that for me the book was spoiled . . . This book is lost
for me on that one count alone. I can never think of it, or look at it, with
anything but shame inside," etc.

That's an epic charge, all right. That one would make the thickest-skinned
man shrink. And I'm not the thickest-skinned man. By all odds I should have
shrunk away to nothing. I turned your insides, shamed you—plastered you with
a nasty and evil "tolerance." Ellery "did a shameful thing, *an unforgivably
intolerant thing*, and for the rest of my life I will shun this book, and what it
stands for, in my mind and heart."

Strong words, Dan. Crushers. Nasty? Evil? Shameful? Unforgivable?
Stomach-turning? For the rest of your life? [. . .]

I know it's going to surprise you, but do you know something, Danny?
You've committed the same crime. Yes, sir. And what's more, you committed it
right in this same book.

Your whole objection is the *place* in which I put the Negro murder. You
admit that you were "willing (sic) to have a Negro murder before Ellery came
into the case, or after," so it's not the fact of a Negro murder, *per se*, that makes
you writhe and squirm and feel ashamed and that spoils the book for you. No,
it's the emphasis I placed on it by making it the murder which decides Ellery to
jump into the investigation. Place, emphasis. It's not one of the crowd—like
O'Reilly, or Abernethy, or Stella Petrucchi. It stands out. That's the crime. It
puts the Negro in a special class in this book. Right?

*Yet when you came to pick the character whose murder was by its position
and emphasis in the story going to stand out at least as much as, if not more
than, the character through whose character Ellery enters the case—when you
came to pick the character whose murder was the instrument which made Ellery
apparently solve the case, you picked the other great "anti"-minority prototype . . .
the JEW!*

Why? Why did you make the Donald Katz murder the instrument of Ellery's—
at that point convincing—solution of the case? You were perfectly right in
including a Jew among the nine New York characters—you could hardly avoid
including a Jew (or a Negro). New York without a Jew (or a Negro) is just not New
York. Dan, the Jews don't want special treatment; they want equal treatment. [. . .]

The social emphasis in the long chapter in which the Inspector relates the
five murders before the Negro murder is sharp and unmistakable; it was that
way in your outline, it was right to be that way, and I wholly agreed with it. The
emphasis was on what the murders were doing to New York—to the people of
New York. Something's going to pop, the Inspector says; something bad—it's
in the air—he doesn't like the way New Yorkers are reacting to these murders;

this is something special; "five murders and anybody would think it was the end of the world!" Clearly, what the Inspector was afraid of was a snapping of morale, disorders—what eventually occurred—panic, citywide in scope. At this point, a Negro is murdered in Harlem. Immediately Ellery says he'll go in. Next page. The Mayor is calling a dawn press conference. "There is no race angle to this murder," he assures the reporters. "What we've got to avoid is the kind of thing that led to the Harlem disorders of 1935," or words to that effect. [. . .] Surely it's clear that to have a riot in Harlem on top of the already explosive nervousness of New York City might blow the lid off the city?

In other words, it's law and order the authorities are concerned about—not concern for Negroes. And when the Inspector paled at the news that a Negro was the sixth victim, and Ellery jumped in—what other conclusion can be drawn except that it was law and order, the state of the public morale, the prevention of a blowup, that made him jump? All through the story Ellery is reacting—and the Inspector—to the state of the public morale. All through the story Ellery is fighting to get a solution before a blowup comes. There's a sense of haste, desperation, fighting against time, in everything Ellery says and does. And for a clearly expressed purpose. Why should people take the view that it was public morale Ellery was concerned about in the Lenore Richardson murder, the Stella Petrucchi murder, and the Donald Katz murder, but pro-Negroism that concerned him in the Beatrice Wilkins-White murder? The proof of my contention is that Ellery could hate and fear Negroes, be another lynch-artist, and not one word of that section of the book would have to be cut or changed!

* * *

It is now three minutes past 5 o'clock in the morning. I've sat here all night writing this letter, since last evening. It's light outside, the birds are chirping, and everybody's happy and rested but me.

What the hell is this all about?

What kind of curse is on you and on me that makes these ridiculous, wasted, bitter, venomous exchanges unavoidable?

Your letter stung me very deeply. I felt it was unfair, deliberately insulting, vehemently unreasonable—and several thousand words of unfairness and insult and unreasonableness are palliated by a last paragraph which states "I have tried to write this letter as dispassionately, as reasonably, as intelligently, as understandingly as I can."

I honestly don't know what to do, what to say about any of the things for Salmen. I don't know now what I have a right not to do, or to do, what I should write Salmen—anything. I do know one thing: I am sicker of the Cat novel than of anything in my entire life—bar none. I didn't think it was possible, but it is. It's hard enough to make a living under the best of circumstances; but to have to do it this way—Shit.

After 2-1/2 hours' sleep

[. . .] There can be only one reason for your acceptance of this double-standard judgment of our respective duties and privileges. You have an utter loathing and contempt for me and my work. I don't "merit" the standards you arrogate to yourself, the standards or its duties and privileges. I'm the inferior; you're the boss. Papa knows best. You have never once in twenty years been able to resist rubbing my nose in the dirt when events have proved me wrong, as they frequently have. You take a joy in my failures, a bitter satisfaction (and not only in my working failures, I might add). We're both bad losers; but you're also a bad winner. And that's one charge I don't think even you can hurl at me. Events have proved you wrong on occasion, too; but I've never crowed over your failures, or crammed them down your throat.

What does all this vomit accomplish? Broad daylight—mid-morning—and the agony and frustration that accompany every such performance.

The hell with it.

MANNY

May 12, 1949

Dear Man:

As I write these words I am taking a sacred oath with myself that never again, under any circumstances whatever, will I write you about the personal aspects of our relationship. After this letter, which I shall try to keep short, and which will in effect be merely a string of denials, my letters to you will be so strictly business, so 100 percent impersonal business, that never again will we have to go through this terrible anguish, this inhuman suffering. I am so physically and mentally ill right now, and I believe you are too, that if it ever happens again, it will be my own damned fault, and I'll deserve it.

If someone told me that after all these years two people could be as far apart in basic understanding, that two people could write each [other] such long letters and yet not achieve even an understanding of what one says to the other—achieve mere understanding, to say nothing whatever of agreement—I would have said it was absolutely impossible. If the situation between us were put into a book, it would be damned as utterly incredible.

There is no point to my writing in reply to all you say. Actually, there is no point in my writing in reply to anything you say. By no point I mean, no possible good will be served, no possible clarification can even be hoped for. [. . .]

I do not want what you call a literal transcription of my outlines. I recognize, and have always recognized, that there must be almost an infinite number of variations, changes, and so on. I do not want or expect a word for word, comma for comma expansion of my outlines. What I do want and expect and think I have the right to expect is simply this: that when you make an *important* change, you at least discuss it with me. But you have not done this. You have made vital changes and I have learned of them only after the manuscript was finished. Is it unreasonable on my part to expect and to ask that you *discuss* important changes in plot, characters, viewpoint? I don't think so; I think it would be good for the finished work to discuss important changes, even if we cannot finally agree; I think it should be compulsory to *discuss* important changes. [. . .]

Surely the Negro change in the cat story could have been *discussed*—I keep underlining the word discussed because I want the emphasis on *discussion*, it being understood obviously that discussion does not mean anything but an exchange of views—it does not imply agreement. [. . .]

With regard to the significance of the Negro murder: you say that I committed the same crime of intolerance, and that I committed it right in this same book. And then you compare the Negro murder and its placement in the story with the so-called Jewish murder and its placement in the story. Manny, if I thought you were right in this matter—even remotely, infinitesimally right—I would never be able to face myself again. I would have to admit that I am a complete fraud, that every drop of blood in my body, that every cell in my body, is thoroughly dishonest.

Can you seriously compare these two murders? Can you seriously maintain that the Katz murder is "the instrument which made Ellery apparently solve the case"? I see no comparison whatever. In the one instance, it is the color of the victim that brings Ellery into the case, where he has refused to enter the case because of another color. In the other instance, what has Jewishness got to do with it? Is Jewishness the instrument which made Ellery apparently solve the case?

In the first place—and this is only a trivial point—the comparison is impossible because of relative positiveness. There is no possible question that the Negro murder concerns a Negro; but the matter is not at all definite in the Katz murder. The Katzes might be Jewish; they might just as easily be non-Jewish Germans. [. . .]

The Negro point is an important instrument in the story, as it affects Ellery; the Jewishness of the name Katz is not an instrument at all.

How you can possibly believe the name Katz and the circumstance of the Katz murder, as I originally outlined them, indicates special treatment to Jews? How in God's name can you seriously make the statement that if Ellery couldn't solve the case after investigating eight Christian murders, he shouldn't solve it after investigating a Jewish murder? The Katz murder is not a *Jewish* murder, and moreover, it is not true to say that Ellery did solve the case at that point.

What the hell . . .

Shall I say, as truthfully, as honestly, as sincerely, as I know how, that I think you are accusing me from a depth of unfairness and untruth the like of which I did not think possible between us? Shall I say it? Will it do any good—even a particle—if I do say it?

Nevertheless, I say it. I say, in as simple and clear language as I know, with nothing but truth in my heart, and in my words, that I have neither loathing nor contempt for your work; I do have honest disagreement, but even you must admit that honest disagreement is everyone's right, even mine. I say that I honestly believe that I have more admiration for you and your work than I think you have for me and my work—but we'll let that go, and stick to positive statements and no comparisons. I say that I do not consider you inferior, and that it is impossible for me to believe I ever will consider you inferior. I say that in all honesty I do not think you are right in accusing me of an "I told you so" attitude. I say that I take no joy whatever in your work-failures, any more than I take any joy whatever in my work-failures. I say that in all honesty I have no bitter satisfaction, or any sweet satisfaction, in whatever other failures you have in your life. [. . .] I now take my oath once more: never again will I enter into a personal discussion of our differences or attitudes or beliefs or hurts or successes or failures—from now on, so help me, my letters will be pure, impersonal business, and nothing else.

DAN

1950: The Origin of Evil

Restricting the content of his letters to pure and impersonal matters of business was an impossible task for Dannay. It was for Lee, as well. *Everything* was taken personally. But it was not all *sturm und drang*, as the next letters show. Before we move on to *The Origin of Evil*, however, a few words about the book that followed *Cat of Many Tails* are in order: *Double, Double* (1950).

The Dannay papers don't contain a great deal of material about *Double, Double*. The fourth adventure of EQ in Wrightsville marks the return to less troubled waters that Lee had requested. It doesn't deal with the death of God or other weighty matters; it shakes no rafters, pushes no boundaries. Ellery undergoes no traumas, no crises of faith. His task, pure and simple—or as simple as a Dannay plot allows—is the solving of a mystery, which in this case is based on the children's rhyme that starts: *Rich man, poor man, beggar man, thief . . . Double*'s plot is driven by another of Dannay's grand manipulators who creates a secret pattern that dictates events—-and is, in the end, overtaken by those events. Lee's prose is agile and effective. The mystery is handled adroitly and the book zips along, but *Double*'s real strength is its vivid portrayal of Wrightsville and its inhabitants. One feels great affection for the town and its people. All in all, *Double, Double* is a straightforward return to form. Perhaps this is why there's relatively little correspondence about it: there just wasn't that much to argue over.

The Origin of Evil finds Ellery back in Hollywood for the first time in a number of years. He is looking for material for a new mystery novel and, as Hollywood has always been a source of the garish and the *outré*, he has taken up temporary residence there. The city has changed in many ways since Ellery's last visit. Television has dealt a body blow to the cinema. The grand, gaudy times are over.

Some things don't change, however. Murders still occur. And Ellery is still asked to solve them. Lovely 19-year-old Laurel Hill intrudes on Ellery's Laurel Canyon perch with an incredible claim. She believes that her father, Leander Hill, a prominent L.A. jeweler, was frightened to death by a dead dog left on the family doorstep.

Ellery is quickly enmeshed in the lives of those affected by the death of Leander Hill: Roger Priam, Hill's partner, a wheelchair-bound tyrant; Delia, Priam's wife, a walking invitation to concupiscence; Crowe Macgowan, Delia's son from her first marriage, a Hollywood hunk who's given up clothes and civilization while he waits in his tree-top abode for the H-Bomb to drop; Mr. Collier, Delia's father, a collector of stamps and butterflies, and the one sane man in a crazy climate; and Alfred Wallace, Priam's male secretary, a suave and mysterious figure whose job description involves sleeping with Mrs. Priam.

Like *Ten Days' Wonder*, *Origin*'s story of murderous revenge is built on a famous (if hidden) structure. This time around, Dannay's taste for the grand conceit is drawn from Charles Darwin. The dead dog, it turns out, was a beagle, which was the name of the ship on which Darwin sailed; the stages of evolution, from eel-like creature to *Homo sapiens*, provide Ellery with the knowledge he needs to interpret the clues, reconstruct past events and identify the killer— twice, in fact: Priam is the putative murderer, but he is only Wallace's cat's paw.

Origin doesn't rise to the level of *Wonder* and *Cat*. It's too many things at once—a Hollywood satire, a treatise on the nature of humankind, and a report on the state of the world as well as a typically clever Queen excursion. Ellery's attraction to the luscious Delia Priam is understandable; but his subsequent revulsion with her for her sexual relations with Wallace strikes the modern sensibility as severely judgmental and hypocritically punitive. Lee was right to be concerned with the treatment's mix of the realistic and the fantastic. The way he bridges the two in *Origin* is not always successful. Hollywood's extravagance and salaciousness seems to have rubbed off on his prose. *Origin* is the most *overheated* of Queen's novels. Still, its audacity is memorable and it never fails to entertain.

We begin with Lee's response to Dannay's outline. The changes Lee made are evident by comparing his questions about the treatment with how he handled those questions in the published novel. The character of Mr. Collier, an example of Californian insanity in the treatment, was transformed into the voice of reason. Collier serves as the voice of the authors, and offers a damning indictment of the cruelty, stupidity and senselessness of human behavior.

Likewise of note is the presence of Inspector Queen in the treatment. He does not appear in the novel, his place being taken by Lieutenant Keats of Hollywood Homicide. These and other examples show us Lee looking for a way into the outline, seeking out the ways he can bring it to life. It's a thoughtful, balanced response to Dannay's outline.

Dannay's thoroughness—his attention to the smallest as well as the largest elements that make up a plot—is demonstrated in his answer to Lee's question about the names of the book's characters. It turns out that the names contribute to *Origin*'s evolutionary conception, and Dannay's explanation provides the correspondence with a rare (and welcome) touch of humor.

Jan. 23 [1950]

Dear Dan:

[. . .] As I see it, what trouble exists between us on this question of fantasy in plot stems from our opposing points of view, and our opposing points of view are largely conditioned for, in each case, our peculiar position and function in the collaboration. I have a drive toward "realism"—conformity to the facts and color of life and the world as we live in it—in story; you have a drive to a sort of "superman" psychology in plot, in which vastness and boldness of conception is nearly everything—the colossal idea, planned to stagger if not bowl over the reader. Since such ideas rarely if ever exist in life, they necessarily lead you, in working out the details of the story, into fantasy in development, too; in fact, the bigger the conception, the more fantastic becomes the story. I then face this plot, with my compulsion toward reality, and the trouble begins. It's not so much that I am naturally "reality-minded" while you are naturally "fantasy-minded," although to some extent—creatively—that is true. I think it's more that, being limited by our working method to doing an outline, after which the problem passes out of your control and you are denied the satisfaction of completion, your creative energy strains to compensate for the denial and packs all it can into your work, to make a brilliant impression that will burst through mere outline and coruscate in the finish despite anything I may do to it. For my part, partly in reaction to this, I unconsciously try to give the impress of something similarly "big" and "impressive" in my part of the job, accounting for the fact that I go in the opposite direction, concentrating on realistic details, literary distinction, etc. We react on each other. In a sense the more successful each of us is in the result of his reaction the more intense the next reaction becomes. This process is also accompanied, on each of our parts, by a feeling of continual, even growing, frustration, since all that our best efforts succeed in accomplishing is to spur the other on to more brilliant efforts in his own milieu. We are like two greyhounds on a circular treadmill; the faster we run away from each other the more speed we give the other.

The Darwinian concept in this story is an excellent example of where our eternal race has taken you. It is a great concept, bold, original, "big"—as a mystery idea well-deserving the nomination for "classic." On the other hand, the bigger the leap the more space in which to fall, as you know as well as I. The idea demands that some character take the successive stages of evolution as the master-plan of his plot against some other character. Within the demands of this necessity you have carefully, sometimes brilliantly, worked out what must follow. While recognizing, even applauding, all this, I still look at the result and I must say, "But how fantastic. Who would—could—do such a thing? Nobody human. It doesn't ring true to life in exactly the proportion in which it is brilliantly conceived. The more brilliant, the less true, the less convincing. Yet I have to write this story in terms of people, in a recognizable 'realistic' background." [. . .]

While I agree with the wisdom of selecting Hollywood as a background for the story (in the common view a "fantastic" place, therefore fit setting for a fantastic story) I question the degree to which you have carried it. Not so much because through your characters you have painted an exaggerated, distorted picture of Hollywood—although that is certainly a consideration—as because, as the reader reads, the "extreme" picture will be backed up by the "extreme" answer, contriving to give an allover impression of "extremeness"—that is, of fantasy whole and unrelieved. This, I think, would be disastrous; the book would seem to have utterly no root in real life. I completely omit consideration of what Ellery's position in such a story would be.

I assume, of course, that it was not your intention to see produced an utter fantasy in all important respects. If I do not assume that, then there is hardly a working basis of discussion.

When I say "an exaggerated, distorted picture of Hollywood," exactly what do I mean? I do not mean of the physical place, because that you have, correctly, not touched on. [. . .] No, in your outline we see Hollywood through its characters. What are its characters? Well, without going into them specifically at this point, they are all "characters"—that is, extremely marked individuals of varying degrees of eccentricity or goofiness, or as in the case of the heroine, of a sort of hardbitten emotionalism. There is little or no relief. The reader cries out for a normal character, for one of the millions of relatively normal people who inhabit this part of the United States . . . that is, for contact with reality. [. . .]

I can only suggest that some attempt be made to cut down the extremeness, where it can be done without damaging the mystery fabric. This is not just to please me. I think it would make a better finished job . . . well, a better-balanced one, anyway. Let me put it this way: Your really central character, Priam, is extreme enough to carry the whole book. He is not merely a cripple chained to a wheelchair which he *never leaves* (for mystery reasons), he is a cripple eternally chained to a wheelchair which is mechanically fitted out to serve as his bed, office, dining table, presumably toilet (and bath?), etc. Incidentally, he also wears a beard, making him visually even more marked. On top of this he is a piratical character, whose every drive is domineering and obsessive—to the absolute extreme. And of top of this, we find out that he is also a pervert—no other characterization is fair to a man who hires ablebodied secretaries not paralyzed from the waist down to sleep with his beautiful wife. (And on top of this we find that, to all intents and purposes, he is the criminal in the story). I submit that this is character enough for six novels.

Ranged beside him is his wife. This is a mature woman of such extraordinary sex appeal that even Ellery can't keep his mind off her. She is cold and purposeful—and morally about as appealing as a guinea pig. She has no qualms, apparently, about sleeping with every man her husband hires, knowing that he is hiring them for the express purpose of laying her. On top of this, she won't leave him "for appearance's sake." A whole book could be written about this woman. She is a character with a vengeance.

Then there is the wife's son by a previous marriage. For a considerable part of the book we find him living in a tree like Tarzan, within a stone's-throw of Hollywood Boulevard, in anticipation of the Atomic Age. The fact that eventually we find out that he was doing it all for publicity, to get into the movies, doesn't fundamentally alter the picture of his screwiness. [. . .]

Finally, among the out-and-out "characters," there is Delia Priam's father, Cap Collier, who is frankly off his chump—not just senile, but extremely so, as evidenced by his behavior on page 35 of the outline—wearing shorts, sweater, straw hat, riding a bicycle, a cigar in his mouth and lollipop over his ear.

Alfred Wallace, who doesn't at all mind accepting his role of Red to Priam's Popeye (remember Faulkner's "Sanctuary"?), is probably the most normal of the cast, although in the end we find that it was his mind that directed the extraordinary events.

Even Laurel Hill, our heroine, is a cool proposition one minute and a hysterical gun-toting female the other. [. . .]

Reviewing what I have already written, it strikes me that you may feel I have overemphasized what I consider the bad things and given insufficient consideration to the good. So I want to say again that I think this job is a *tour de force* and in many ways the most brilliant you have ever done. Even as far as the characters are concerned, I have no objection to Priam, or Delia, or any of the others, as individual characters; I am even impressed with one or two of them. It is just that I feel there are too many of them and that their numbers and the emphasis their numbers give force a distortion in the allover feel of the book, which needs more balance. Please remember this when reading my specific comments, questions, and suggestions. Obviously they will all be in the nature of objections of disagreements with what you have; there is no time or need to go similarly into those things which I either do not object to or agree with wholeheartedly.

* * *

I had better transcribe my notes as I've made them, without attempting to classify them according to type. Some will be questions for clarification, others will raise questions of other sorts, etc.

(1) The question of the names. Somewhere you made a special note to me to be careful about "changing" any of the names as there was some plan or purpose behind most of them—I'm not sure where your note was and I don't want to take the time dig it out now. Just what did you mean by that warning and how far did you intend your warning to be a prohibition? Of course I recognize the necessity of retaining "Alfred Wallace." On the other hand, I confess I don't see the point that apparently exists behind the other names, and I would like to know what it is. I may have a thought about it, as in the case of "Leander Hill," for instance, I don't cotton much to "Leander"; it seems to me forced, especially in juxtaposition to "Priam"—both coming out of Greek legend. If this was part of what you had in mind, I don't get the point. If not, I'd like to know what the point was. [. . .]

(2) Why is the Inspector in this story? The only function I could find that he serves is as an ear to Ellery at certain points; and if that is the only reason he is in, or the only important reason, I think he can be dispensed with. In the first place, once Keats enters the story Keats can be Ellery's ear (as he is for the most part, anyway). In the second place, the Inspector seems like a fish out of water. He does nothing indispensable; for a large part of the story the outline doesn't even mention him. Nothing that I can see is gained by retaining him for the father-son relationship, which has no bearing on the story in any detail or mood. Besides, I have the feeling the story will be better off having Ellery in it as a lone wolf, unencumbered by a personal relationship. [. . .]

(3) As the outline now has it, Laurel and Delia both come to Ellery to employ him on the same day. This struck me as a wholly unnecessary coincidence, which certainly should be fixed if it can be. And it can be. If Ellery's stay in Hollywood had been attended by local publicity, then there is a valid reason why people seeking detectival help should come to him on one another's heels. What do you think?

(4) *Page 1.* Laurel tells Ellery the curious incident of her father's receipt of a dead dog, an anonymous gift—"some sort of hunting dog" with a collar on which is a silver box, containing a message of some sort. Later, she says, after her father's heart attack, when she sought the dog, she found it had been carted off "by the Sanitation Department." Ellery's concern with this incident, until late in the story when he gets around to asking her to identify the exact breed of hunting dog and gets the beagle answer, is restricted in the outline wholly to the

message which has disappeared. When he finds Leander's transcript of the message his interest in the incident apparently lapses.

It seems to me Ellery is guilty here of a serious omission. The first questions that occurred to me, the answers to which I look for and failed to find anywhere, were: *How* was the dog received? Had it been mailed? Boxed? Just left on the doorstep? What kind of hunter was it? (All right, this one must be left unsaid until the proper time.) [. . .] How could Ellery avoid trying to trace the owner of the dog? How could he avoid searching for the missing collar as well as the missing message?

(5) The question of Priam's wheelchair raises corollary questions I have already touched on. (Page 8.) If Priam "has not left the wheelchair in 15 years"—literally—how did he dress and undress? How did he crap and piss? How did he bathe? That he did not leave the wheelchair at any time—ever—night or day—is a must; and the more mandatory it becomes, the more fascinating become the speculations about his primary functions. I don't think they should intrude, and the simplest way to keep them from intruding is to suggest the answer. [. . .]

(6) Old Cap Collier. This character brings up the whole question of character extremeness and the lopsided picture of Hollywood that I mentioned earlier. [. . .] Collier stuck in my craw from the beginning as representing the element that tipped the scales way over. I think a great deal of the outbalance can be removed—and this is a seriously intended suggestion—if Collier is changed from what he is in the outline to a supremely sane man—as normally sane a man as he can be made. He can retain a sane man's hobbies and interests; perhaps he has something of a scientific background. I would like to see him a quiet observer of all that is going on, minding his own business, offering no information, pursuing his quiet hobbies, but in a sane and reasonable way rather than as now, and in appearance and habits as normal as possible—a retired citizen of California, an old man, living out his life here—typical of hundreds of thousands of such people, especially in Southern California, who have come here to die in the so-called sunshine. The saner and more uncommunicative he is, the better balance he will be for the others, by sheer contrast; and by that fact he will become, although this is of no great importance, a good dark herring. His hobbies can be retained along the botanical and biological lines. [. . .]

(7) *Page 13.* As it stands now, Laurel "remembers" her father's diary habit only after Ellery's fruitless search for the message. Her recollection at just the right moment—after letting Ellery knock himself out looking for the message—seems to me to over-convenient. It's a very small point, but I suggest that after Ellery has unsuccessfully sought for the message, he questions Laurel closely and it is through his questioning that her recollection of his diary comes out.

(8) *Page 25.* After the frogs incident: Ellery and Keats "talk things over at headquarters." It seems to me almost the first thing they would have to "talk

over" is how the strewer of the dead frogs got into Priam's house, at what time exactly, etc., in addition to why he selected frogs as the third warning, etc. [. . .]

(9) *Page 29.* The question of the background of Priam and Hill, as brought out in the resume *vis-à-vis* Ellery and Keats. The chronology here may be of some importance, and at any rate the question I raise makes necessary further material to be at least touched on in the resume. If Priam was paralyzed for 15 years, that is, 15 years ago, and was paid off, after investigation, "by no less than six insurance companies" which "authenticated the paralysis", when were those policies taken out? You say the police could not dig up any information about Priam and Hill dating "prior to their coming to Los Angeles about 20 years ago." This having to be the case, obviously then Priam's policies are no more than, at the outside, 20 years old—are, in fact, between fifteen and twenty years old. Because policies older than 20 years would contain information about Priam in his pre-Priam personality, so to speak, and would leave a trail you don't want left. [. . .]

(10) *Page 34.* The alligator wallet. Keats would, as one of his first acts in this connection, want to fingerprint that wallet. This obviously should not be. Therefore Priam should refuse to let Keats have the wallet.

(11) This is out of its proper place, but since the whole question I raise spreads more or less throughout the major part of the book, it hardly matters where I raise it. It concerns Ellery's reactions to Delia. As you delineated them, they disturbed me constantly. But when I got to the fact that Ellery began to feel "guilty feelings" about Delia, I put my finger on the cause. In the first place, for what Delia has revealed herself as, Ellery can only feel contempt. She takes a life of crud from Priam daily, yet she stays with him "for appearance's sake." She had no objection whatever, from anything I can find to the contrary, to sleeping with Alfred at Priam's arrangement, or with any of the other men who preceded Alfred in the Priam establishment. So, as a person, she is weak and vicious, and I simply can't see Ellery having "guilty feelings" about his thoughts in relation to her. He is attracted to her? Okay, but how can it be for any but purely sexual reasons? All right, he feels a yen for her. The only possible basis for having "guilty feelings" in this connection is because he is disappointed in *himself.* But I'd rather he didn't have guilty feelings at all. I'd rather he was just surprised at himself, maybe a little wryly amused. Anything else, Delia being what she is, would strike me as being pretty adolescent. As to his reactions to Alfred, they should be no more than a sort of jungle sexual jealousy, if anything—and he can be amused at himself in this connection, too. Actually, I haven't put this in the proper chronology. I think Ellery's feelings should show a definite rise and fall. In the beginning, when he first meets her, he is attracted to her sexually, but suspects she is not all she should be as a person. When he finds out that Alfred is laying her (page 31) and, what is more, with Priam's acquiescence, if not encouragement—a situation which all three are quite aware

of—Fllery's reaction should be pure disgust. I don't see how he could react any other way, and any sex feelings he had for Delia would, it seems to me, die like a hard-on plunged in cold water. I'd hate to think he reacted any other way! In a way, this thread could constitute a sort of "Education of E.Q." in the Faulknerian aspects of Hollywood life.

(12) This one, I admit, stumps me. It concerns the clue of the worthless stock certificates, the conclusion from which is that they constitute, in the vernacular, "cats and dogs." Dan, this struck me as awfully strained, the only one of the clues which did. It is difficult for me to visualize a man concocting a plot in which successive elements of evolution had to be deduced by a detective and utilizing as one of his clues-to-be-seen-through worthless-stock-certificates-meaning-"cats-and-dogs". [. . .]

(13) Adam and his "hundred million dollars." This struck me, at the time I first encountered it, as wholly unnecessary—I mean, the size of the fortune. Of course, when I had got to the end I saw the reason for it. [. . .]

(13) *Page 54.* There is a small point here about Ellery's apparent willingness to let Priam go unguarded after Ellery's warning of death to Priam, even though we later discover it was part of Ellery's plan to catch Priam. [. . .] This is bound to make the reader disappointed in Ellery. I merely note it for my own reference at the proper time, as somehow I will have to handle this to satisfy all the factors involved. [. . .]

(14) *Page 62.* Ellery reconstructing Priam's motive to kill Hill: It seems to me that you have constructed a needlessly complicated business here. [. . .] It seems to me simpler and more believable all around if the following was the situation: Priam, because he was paralyzed, and against all the dictates of his nature, was forced to sit by and watch while Hill, who was physically unimpaired, for that reason was in active charge of their business. Priam's need to dominate was therefore frustrated in this connection for many years. So Priam plotted Hill's death *in order to gain sole operational control of the business*, and not for financial reasons at all. This, it seems to me, is a completely consistent development of Priam's overwhelming compulsion to dominate and is therefore much better integrated into the story. And by the time Ellery "reconstructs," I think Priam's domineering character will have been so firmly established that the motive will seem not merely plausible, but inevitable. What do you think?

(15) *Page 66.* Three months after the "conclusion" of the case, we find Alfred working for Ellery. Nothing is said of Alfred's part in the trial of Priam, or that he *had* any part in the trial. [. . .]

(16) *Page 67.* Referring to my point (2)—the Inspector's being in the story—if you agree that the Inspector can be left out, then his place as the "ear" in this section beginning at the bottom of p. 67 can be taken by Keats, who has dropped in on Ellery. Keats can drop in with exactly the same objections you put

in the Inspector's mouth. In fact, I think coming from Keats, an outsider, the question will have more force and point and interest and to that extent will make the whole payoff better.

(17) *Page 72*. I am troubled here, last paragraph of the page. [. . .] I can see no reason for Priam to tell Alfred the background story, I can see no way in which Alfred could ostensibly have got hold of the story in order to be able to suggest it to Priam—and still it is necessary for the plot that Alfred "learn" the background story in a way which will not make Priam suspicious. [. . .]

(18) *Page 76*. Last two lines of main story. In one of your points in your note which I was to read after reading the outline, you say that these last two lines "will bear discussion." Apparently you have some doubt about the advisability of using this device. If you have, I share it. I am against the author's stepping out of the book to address a direct question to the reader. We gave up CHALLENGE TO THE READER years ago as an outmoded device; I see no reason to get back into that cycle. [. . .] But when Alfred smiles on page 305, or whatever it is, that ought to be the end of Queen's book.

As to Alfred's not saying a word throughout that last scene, it strikes me at this time as a pretty good device; but I can't predict how it will feel at the time I get to it, so I had rather leave the question open. [. . .]

ABOUT THE TITLE: I think I have previously indicated that the title, *The Origin of Evil*, did not—to answer your question—"tip me off" and that I did not see through the gimmick. I still feel that, while I like *The Origin of Evil* well enough as a title, I do not like it as the title of a Queen novel, as it doesn't give me enough of a mystery-novel feeling; as I think I said, it sounds more like a Queen anthology of some sort, certainly very much like the title of a non-fiction book. The very word "origin" which ties it up to Darwin's work is the word that gives it this non-fiction feeling, and I felt that even before I knew anything about the Darwinian parallelism. [. . .]

I have a suggestion which is, in its own way, more daring than *The Origin of Evil*, at least insofar as a connection with Darwin is concerned. It is a phrase that has come to be associated with the theory of evolution; but it has this further advantage, that is it is phrase also commonly used in detective lore and literature. If it were to be used as the title of a story by Ellery Queen, it would instantly be assumed that its meaning concerns its lay association—that is, its criminal connotation. And Ellery could, throughout the book, be looking for "it," calling it by the phrase which would be the book's title.

That is: *The Missing Link*.

Look at the advantages. *The Missing Link* has a detective-story connotation in combination with the Queen name. It is a phrase—its hidden significance—associated with the theory of evolution. What is more, by definition the phrase "the missing link" connotes the *search for a man*—the hypothetical man-organism linking ape to man. In every way it strikes me as peculiarly felicitous, especially since Ellery can use the phrase easily and naturally. Somewhere in the outline, for instance, Ellery has the feeling that he is overlooking something, that something which ties everything together—the usual Ellery-approach. This is where his use of the phrase "the missing link" could come in with the greatest naturalness and the least suspicion as to its true meaning. I don't think there's a chance in the world anyone will tie it up to the gimmick of the story—even if he should happen to think of it in its evolutional sense. I think the gimmick is so deeply concealed as to be beyond discovery.

Well, this letter has been weeks in the brewing and days in the making, and today I find myself reduced to a whisper—the cold has attacked my vocal chords for a change—and generally feeling like the wrath of God. I'll wrap it up and send it on to you and await development. [. . .]

Kaye is going to have another baby. This was confirmed for us yesterday by the doctor. She is about two months' gone and the approximate date is August 30th. This will neatly coincide with an income tax payment and my heaviest month of the year for insurance premiums. Well planned! We are tightening our belts with a vengeance and there will be no "luxury" expenditures this year—there will be no money for such. I am trying hard not to think—about anything. [. . .]

MANNY

The baby mentioned above was never born; Kaye Brinker Lee suffered a miscarriage. The next addition to the Lee family took place in March 1951, when Rand B. Lee was born.

Jan 27, 1950

Dear Man:

I have your long letter re the new novel—if your letter had been written single-spaced, it would almost have the proportions of an outline, in length— and I'll begin by trying to answer all your questions. On first reading, I see nothing of critical importance—that is, nothing that presents insurmountable, or even very great, difficulties. One of the reasons for this is that I had already arrived at certain changes that pretty well match some of your more serious objections. [. . .]

Although I still think *The Origin of Evil* is the perfect title, I see your points. Readers might easily interpret it as nonfictional, and yes, it might easily seem to be an anthology title. So, despite the fact that I like the title so much, I agree it should be discarded.

I have been thinking of a new title in off moments since you first voiced your objections, and I have something to offer. But first, your own suggestion,

The Missing Link. I like the title except for two objections. First, I think if you asked people what does the phrase *The Missing Link* suggest, the overwhelming majority, if not all, would reply—ape, or gorilla. And not go beyond that. The conception, or connotation, of ape or gorilla is, I feel, all wrong for this book—even though, as you say, the phrase has other meanings and even though, as you say, it has a tie-in with the theory of evolution. Despite all this, I feel that the ape or gorilla "picture" is actually irrelevant. Also, I don't get the reaction from this title of dignity or bigness, and I think the title of this book should have a serious, dignified, big feeling.

However, let's not rule it out; let me try to get used to it, or see how it wears with me. [. . .]

Next, about the character names. [. . .] I was having fun, and I wondered if you would see through it. I wanted to know if my peculiar kind of fun was obvious, and the fact that you did not see what I had in mind proves that it was not obvious at all. But I wanted to be sure that you didn't change names without at least realizing the fun I was having with the names I gave you. [. . .]

Here is what I had in mind, and if you do not like it, of course change the names; but the fact that you didn't see it for yourself might persuade you to go along—even with the knowledge that virtually no readers would see the hidden significance—the fun that the authors are having.

Leander Hill is close to—Neanderthal

Mr. and Mrs. Priam are—Priam-mates, or Primates

Crowe Macgowan is close to—Cro-magnon

They are remarkably appropriate, aren't they? Okay, so I'm having fun.

The other names do not follow this pattern at all. [. . .]

Now, to other matters in rough order of your letter.

There seems to be no point in discussing our relative "realistic" and "fantastic" drives, except perhaps for me to make a few comments, purely for what they may be worth. Despite the kind of plots I have been giving you recently, I think I am much more of a realist than you are willing to admit. Remember, Man, that it was I who broke away from our own past to plot *Calamity Town* and to begin the saga of Wrightsville, with all that meant in *Calamity Town* and *The Murderer is a Fox*. Remember, too, Man, that it was I who broke away from fantasy-in-Wrightsville (*Ten Days' Wonder*) to *Cat of Many Tails*. Neither breakaway was prompted by you—at least, in any direct or dogmatic way. But every time I broke away to comparative realism, we ran into trouble between ourselves. You would make changes, without even bothering to discuss them with me until it was too late; or, as in the case of *Calamity Town*, you didn't like the plot at all—or don't you recall that? [. . .]

I don't honestly think we can do a really realistic novel in the detective field—not what I call realism. Also, Man, I honestly think that there is more realism in a good fantasy than in bad realism. [. . .]

While I am giving a few views on realism-versus-fantasy, perhaps I should bring up the matter of the *next* novel. I cannot tell you how tired I am now—enormously so. I could not start on a new novel for some time. I have been doing advance work on the magazine, in order to be able to take Steve to Cleveland for an operation, if the doctors so decide. I don't know how long the operation will keep us in Cleveland, but I must be prepared for whatever time is required. Steve is not well—which is a definite understatement. The fact is, Man, I cannot write to you about Steve—I cannot bring myself to. Bill and I are hoping, praying—that is all I can say.

But sooner or later, I must start a new novel. And what to do? I had already decided—long before your last letter—that I would not do anything even remotely like what you call fantasy. I am through with that—not because I think it is wrong, but because it continues the heartbreaking trouble between us. [. . .]

To digress for a moment: *The Origin of Evil* (to refer to it by its original title) was done last summer—at a time, Man, when I was tremendously troubled—emotionally, mentally, over Steve—and when I was very ill myself, losing a pound a day regularly, and being virtually blind. The miracle is that I was able to work at all. That I produced what I believe to be a remarkable story—I am aware of its peculiar brilliance—was perhaps somehow due to the very circumstances under which it was born. The strain, pressure, illness, blindness, even hopelessness, drove me, or perhaps even inspired me—who knows? But at that cost I would not last long. [. . .]

Also, and I know I have said this before, there is one more thing you should not, in my opinion, ever lose sight of. I don't know how good or bad a realistic detective story we could do; but I will say this: there is no one in the field—no one—who can do the sort of thing Queen is known for. Who else in the field could do *The Origin of Evil*? If you grant this, then you must ask yourself: shouldn't Queen continue to do what Queen readers have come to expect from Queen? Fantasy, of the Queen type, is not a common commodity. How much is it worth to us to continue this approach, providing we are different-from-all-others and providing that difference gives Queen some stamp of individuality? [. . .]

It seems to me that Hollywood is not only the natural place, but perfect place for this story. As to its being extreme, again I must bow to your judgment—after all, you are closer to it than I am. But I still think you underestimate what people outside of Hollywood think or know of the place. Hollywood has not reformed so much in the last ten years that it has completely lost its reputation for being the home of screwballs and crackpots. What I'm trying to say is that even after you have raised the point, I am not really disturbed by it. The story does not have to be billed as a cross-sectional picture of Hollywood; it is about these particular people, and they are what they are (more of this later). If there is exaggeration and distortion, it is not Hollywood as a whole—no attempt is being made to portray Hollywood as such; the story portrays these people living in Hollywood. Also, exaggeration is the tool of satire, and accepted as such; and surely you realize that there is a good deal of satire in the story.

By the way, just as an interjection: Are the Chandler stories, whose characters are uniformly more vicious and, in my opinion, more exaggerated and distorted, typical Hollywood stories? Yet Chandler's stories are supposed to be laid in Hollywood. [. . .]

As I have already indicated, the Inspector was my nomination for the "sane man" in the story. More, he represented Ellery's refuge from a mad world around him. Besides being Ellery's "ear," he is also Ellery's anchor, balance-wheel—and that, ironically, when the Inspector is ill and convalescing! But if you wish, I have no objection to your eliminating the Inspector entirely. I think something would be lost—the Inspector always adds, or can add, to Ellery's humanity; the Inspector in the background always has the tendency to make Ellery more of a human being. But I am perfectly willing for you to make this decision—whether to keep the Inspector or remove him altogether from this story. [. . .]

I think it is very important that Laurel and Delia not only come to consult Ellery on the same day, but on the heels of each other. It is important that they meet in Ellery's presence in the very first chapter—so that the secret enmity, as well as the contrast in their characters, hits the reader immediately—so that this secret enmity, culminating in the climactic scene between the two of them (the shooting of Delia by Laurel) begins at once, in Ellery's presence, and continues throughout the story whenever they meet. The secret enmity, of course, is compounded of the contrast in their characters, of Laurel's reaction to the kind of woman and life Delia represents, and of Crow, whom they both are attached to and want in entirely different ways. Delia's reaction to Laurel's hysterical shooting of her, despite Delia's admitted amorality (or, if you prefer, immorality) and curiously intertwined conventionalism (her inability to leave Priam "for appearance's sake"), is almost monstrously mature. If you would feel better about their coming to Ellery on the heels of each as the result of publicity attendant upon Ellery's living in Hollywood, okay with me—*but they should visit Ellery in the first chapter on the heels of each other.* [. . .]

Now, about the dog and collar: the vital thing here is that any investigation of the dead dog and the collar should lead nowhere—whether that investigation is made by Ellery or Keats. There must be no clue—in the beginning, and until Ellery has Laurel identify the breed of dog. Thus, I saw the dog merely left in front of the door. If you would rather the dead body of the dog be boxed, okay— but I don't think it is necessary. I saw the dog obtained from some remote and untraceable source, but if you would rather it were stolen, okay. But the trail must lead nowhere. [. . .] The dog's exact breed is never mentioned for the perfectly simple and satisfactory reason that no one—not even Ellery—ever has reason to question the breed, or to think that the breed is of any importance whatever—until Ellery, later, sees that importance. [. . .]

Man, there are thousands of half-paralyzed and wholly paralyzed people in the world—people paralyzed far more than Priam is. Yet they all get along, they all piss and crap. Here again, I did not think it necessary to go into detail. I visualized, for example, an arrangement of the seat, and under the seat, of the wheelchair that would permit certain bodily functions—but it is not necessary to explain this. Priam would be dressed and bathed, or sufficiently helped, by Alfred—that is a male-nurse's job. [. . .] The vital point is that Priam has not left his wheelchair in 15 years—and this is not at all incredible, or unbelievable in any way. Such a situation occurs in every city of the world daily. [. . .]

I had visualized the data in Priam's insurance policies as phoney. As I understand it, the only data that will invalidate insurance policies are lies and deception about the insured's physical condition, and as I understand it, even these will not invalidate a policy after it has been in force a certain number of years. But rather than check this, I see a far better way of handling this situation. *Cut all reference to Priam's insurance policies.* [. . .]

Ellery's reaction to Delia. I think your analysis is right, except for one thing: I don't see Ellery merely surprised at himself, and then amused, either wryly or any other way. I see Ellery angry at himself, kicking himself—a more powerful emotion than mere amusement or surprise. Ellery's reaction to Delia is 100 percent physical, sexual: obviously, there is nothing ethereal, spiritual, or esthetic about it. It is plain maleness reacting to femaleness. Yes, Ellery has guilty feelings—because he is disappointed in himself. He knows Delia for what she is—yet he can't prevent himself from wanting her, or prevent himself from acting like an adolescent in his purely physical attraction to Delia and hurt when she pays no attention to him. Yes, his jealousy is exactly what you say: jungle sexual jealousy. Yes, too, Ellery's feelings should rise and fall—I am quite sure I indicated this in the outline. I am sure too that I indicated his attraction when he first meets Delia, and his disgust (I think I called it revulsion) when he learns beyond suspicion that Alfred is laying her. All this, you will admit, is "new stuff" for Ellery, and you must of course handle it carefully. But it's human as man himself—that's why I feel strongly that Ellery should not be merely amused. Amusement is a sort of intellectual reaction to the situation, and in this instance Ellery should not be intellectual. He'd be damned annoyed with himself, and ashamed of himself—hence, his guilty feelings. [. . .]

If you decide to drop the Inspector, of course it should be Keats who takes part in the last scene, raising the objections that the Inspector now makes. [. . .]

By the way, I have never read Faulkner's *Sanctuary*—so I do not understand your references to it (page 4, near bottom, of your letter). Please explain what you mean. [. . .]

I honestly think, Man, that this book can be a milestone—not only for us, as a spectacular book, but also in the detective-mystery field itself. It is a staggering conception, and even now, months after the fact so far as I am personally concerned, I am still staggered by it. I don't have to tell you that it was an extraordinarily difficult plot to work out, and that I sweated blood on it under the most trying circumstances. But it's done, and now that I think I have ironed out some of the matters that troubled you, and agreed to other matters involving important changes that you will be much happier about, I hope you will be able to do your end with relative peace of mind, and much more important, with a deep enthusiasm for something that can, and should, turn out to be really big. I don't mean to oversell the book to you—if anything, I deliberately *under*sold it when I first sent you the outline—but here is a detective novel to conjure with, here is a real classic. [. . .]

Let me know your thoughts on your own time problems and work schedule, so that I can at least try to synchronize with you.

All other matters, including personal ones, in my next.

DAN

Thursday, Feb. 2 [1950].

Dear Dan:

[. . .] I am still not in entire agreement with you on Ellery's reaction to Delia. You are taking his animal-attraction to her as basic, irrespective of other things about her and unchangeable by finding out still others. I can't get myself to see Ellery that way; not Ellery. While he might easily be attracted to a woman for pure animal reasons, I can only see those feelings lasting up to a certain point. When what she really is comes out—and what she really is is, to me anyway, brutally disgusting—it seems to me Ellery's yen for her physically would be affected. Ellery is not and never has been the kind of guy whose basic drives are unaffected by considerations of filth, vice, etc [. . .] Every man—nearly every man—gets an occasional yen for an unusually sexy woman; those who are screwed up get guilt feelings about it, those who aren't either go after the woman or pass her by, depending on what kind of men they are. So he had a yen. He didn't do anything about it, did he? Then he finds out she's dirt...Well, let's let this go and see how it works out in the finish. It will probably cause me trouble and we will probably in the end disagree about the way it's been done, but I'll try to do it in a way that will somehow satisfy both of us basically. [. . .]

Faulkner's *Sanctuary*? Rather surprised you never read it, since I know you are familiar with his work and *Sanctuary* is certainly one of his standout novels. (He has confessed, by the way, to having written it purely and simply for money, early in his career when he couldn't get to first base with stuff he considered worthy of himself.) It is a grim, gruesome, devastating novel of Mississippi, with probably the lowest set of characters in all fiction. Popeye is a sinister big-city-piece of anthropomorphic scum who sets out, in his Juggernaut fashion, to lay the 17-year old girl who by accident wanders into his life. He does so, in one of the most brutal scenes in all fiction, and—since Faulkner wrote this book very much in the mystery-technique—it is only later in the book, as a climax, that you discover he didn't really lay her at all—he is incapable. What he did was screw her with a corn husk. (Are you there, Sharlie?) But the point I made about Red was this: Later, Popeye takes the girl away and puts her tenderly in a whore house run by a Madam he knows, not to be used for the regular trade but simply for his own "pleasure." Apparently the corn husk technique palls, because he gets a gambler he knows, named Red, a big husky guy, to come up with him to the girl's room in the whore house and lay her for him while he stands by the bed enjoying it . . . vicariously. As a curious index to Popeye's "code," when the girl later shows signs that *she* enjoys Red's attentions, Popeye bumps him neatly off (or has him bumped off, I don't remember which). Anyway, I was reminded of Popeye and Red when I read your outline—Priam hiring secretaries to sleep with his wife, the only difference being that Priam apparently doesn't take a bedside seat for the performance. Does that answer your question? [. . .]

The only thing remaining is your comment about little Steve, which leaves so much unsaid. I am the first to understand how painful the subject must be to you. I can only hope that things are not nearly so bad as they seem to be. In this, needless to say, Kaye joins me most earnestly. Also needless to say, if there is anything we can do which would in any way help matters, in any way at all, let us know.

Kaye is feeling well and—thank God—eating like a horse. She has been very thin, painfully so. The doctor finds her in perfect shape and there should be no trouble with this pregnancy. It will be her last, on that we are agreed. I suppose I reveal no secret when I say we're both hoping it's a girl. Our love to Bill and the boys –

MANNY

Feb 20, 1950

Dear Man:

I have been receiving your letters of increasing woe, and each time I finish one of your letters I can't help asking: what will happen next? I hope by this time everybody is on the mend—Kaye, whose coughing and susceptibility to lung trouble should certainly be checked thoroughly, and Kit's ear trouble, which should also be watched most carefully.

Perhaps I should tell you more of my own troubles. Indeed, I can no longer avoid it, since in this past week something has happened that has compelled me to change all my work plans, and of course you should know of this. First, about

Steve. I don't know how much Helen wrote to you, but I can give you a clear picture by telling you that last Christmas Day the doctors told us that they did not expect Steve to live more than a month or so. That was our Christmas present. It is now well over a month, and Steve has actually improved. What the improvement means, we don't know; whether is temporary or not, we don't know. He has been getting insulin injections for about a month, and there is no doubt that his improvement dates from the beginning of the insulin injections. Bill gives the injections, and if you and Kaye cannot find the heart to jab Kit, what of Bill—especially when I tell you that there is hardly any flesh on Steve into which the needle can be plunged.

The doctors are aware that in the past month Steve has improved: he is more alert, more active, less nervous, sleeps better, and generally looks better; he has gained a wee bit of weight, but he still weighs considerably less than he did one year ago (which gives you some idea of the last year). The doctors refuse to commit themselves. The truth is, they do not know what is precisely the matter with Steve, except that they are all agreed that it is something in the brain.

For the last year and a half Bill and I have taken a terrific beating. Now we live from day to day, not daring to look ahead to the day after. I have tried to steel myself, so that if I seem cold and remote, so far as your troubles are concerned, it is only because I keep desperately trying to maintain as objective an attitude as it is possible for me. Up to this past week I have been working very hard—long hours and grueling concentration; but this has frankly been a form of running away, and of course I know it. I have been trying to keep myself so occupied that I have a minimum of time to think ahead.

But something happened last week that forced me to readjust all my thinking and all my plans. Early last week we had our first heavy snowfall—six inches. I went out and shoveled the front walk and the back stairs. When I came into the house, I was seized with a dizzy spell, and for two days I was flat on my back. Now I am up, though still dizzy at times, and am suffering from a lousy cold—eyes streaming, nose running, the works. The dizziness? I don't know. I thought that perhaps I had had a slight heart attack, resulting from the exertion of shoveling; but the doctor says no. But while I lay on my back, I began to think.

As you know, I was very ill this summer. The deep anxiety over Steve brought on an acute attack of diabetes, with resultant near-blindness. I am no longer taking insulin, although I check my urine every day. But my sugar varies, and with the ups and downs I have a fluctuating ability to see—some days good, other days bad. Right at this moment, as I type, my eyesight is quite poor. The point is that I believe Bill and I are dangerously close to physical breakdowns. I don't have to tell you that Bill is perfectly wonderful, but even she can't go indefinitely, with what hangs over us from day to day, without let-up.

Then, too, we must consider the older boys. They have taken Steve's constant illness with remarkable understanding; but you can't have the kind of situation we have been living through without suffering inside.

So, while on my back, I came to the conclusion that Bill and I must do something to protect our health and the older boys' health. Needless to tell you, we are doing all in our power to help Steve, and will go, if necessary, anywhere, to see anyone, if it will help. We are, with regard to Steve, in the doctor's hands, and in God's.

I have determined to close up the house this summer and rent a house somewhere else—perhaps on Cape Cod, or perhaps in Maine. We must get away, have a change—for what little good it may do. I plan to take the maid and the nurse with us, and of course the children, and have a new background for the summer months. The doctors have agreed to let us take Steve away, as long as we are near a big city—Boston, or Cape Cod, for example. As to the money it will cost, I figure our expenses away will be about the same as they are here— food, maid, nurse, etc. The extra cost will be the rental of a furnished house, and I hope to get one for, say, $1000, including transportation. [. . .]

In order to go away as soon as school closes, I have to prepare an extra four issues of the magazine. [. . .] So, as soon as I feel better, I am going to plunge back into magazine work. It means really six issues—two between now and the next deadline, and four to carry through until the end of the summer. Meanwhile, Bill is trying to get a line on a house somewhere. Of course, other things can happen: if Steve should take a sudden turn—but we can only plan.

I can prepare the magazine work that far in advance, then I can devote the summer months to making a start at least on the next novel. I am going to try to work it out so that I will have virtually all my summer time—at least, as much as possible—for the next novel. [. . .]

You said in your latest letter that despite the emergency in your house you simply couldn't afford to hire a nurse. Manny, is that true? Do you really mean that you cannot hire a nurse for a week or two in a sickness emergency—that is, that your reserves are so far gone, so far depleted, that a nurse's wages for a week or two are out of the question?

I must say (and perhaps I have no right to comment) that this frightens me. Why are you that low? Have you had some big expense that I know nothing of? I ask these questions not to be nosy, not merely to satisfy pure curiosity on my part, but because I am genuinely concerned. I know what we are both earning; in fact, I realize at times your income is even more than mine—those times that Kaye takes radio work. [. . .]

Man, if you are that low, with no reserves at all left, what would happen in an even bigger emergency? Suppose our income suddenly went to pot? Suppose one of us got incapacitated? What would you do? [. . .]

I know that you have been borrowing money through Curtis Brown, and Man, I am genuinely concerned. How can we possibly assume that our income will even remain at its present level? Of course, we can try our best, not only to maintain it, but to increase it; but surely you know the precarious nature of our business. Good God, suppose something went wrong with the magazine! It could happen, Man, despite my most conscientious efforts.

If you would rather not discuss this with me, I will understand. But if you could give me some inkling of your problem—of that part of the problem of which I do not know—at least I would not worry about it in the dark, so to speak. [. . .]

I'm pooped and am getting into bed with aspirin and Vicks. I wish I had something really cheerful, really encouraging, to say in six solid pages of single-spaced typing, but if I have, I can't think of it . . .

DAN

Friday Feb. 24 [1950].

Dear Dan:

I have no heart or mind, almost no body, to answer your letter; still, it has to be answered.

Nobody really understands anyone else's troubles. For those of us who are excessively troubled—and that includes both of us—the lack of understanding is compounded by a concentration on self which isn't so much selfishness as self-centeredness, a preoccupation with self, which only deepens the fog and builds the wall higher. It is of no use to say, Think of others first. Forget yourself. It can't be done. One's own troubles are in the forefront and the troubles of others are in the rear, pushing forward only at intervals and for short times, and then falling back again.

So it is with you and me. I appreciate and sympathize with your troubles, but I am preoccupied with my own. You appreciate and sympathize with mine, but you are preoccupied with yours.

Nor is it of the slightest value to attempt to weigh one's troubles against another's and say, Mine are less than his, or mine are more. One can say it, but the saying means nothing. To every man his own. A trouble of mine which to you might seem trifling to me might seem elephantine. A trouble of yours which to me might have little significance to you might be of the greatest importance.

Our troubles lie deeper than family illness, as serious as family illness has been, especially to you. I do not minimize, believe me, what you and Bill have been going through with Stevie. I suppose I need hardly have said that. Nor being faced with such a situation, I can hardly attempt to evaluate what my reaction would be if such a thing were to strike in this house. I might—probably would—react far less courageously than you and Bill. But if that were so, it would only be because I am possibly a little more screwed up. It isn't what happens to us, it's the way we react to it, that's of importance. Our childhood and adolescence are a long preparation for coping with the exigencies of life; in my case, at least, the preparation was muddled and poor, to the extent that I have at last come to the end of . . . well, one of the ropes. But more of that later.

As to your news about Stevie and his apparent response to insulin, I can only join with Kaye in hoping with you and Bill that you have at last struck something hopeful, therapeutic, and of permanent value. I can't project myself, I can only imagine—and that inadequately—what all this is doing to you, this unremitting worry, nervous drain, shock, etc. Keep up your strength. Don't give up hope. Grit your teeth. It is the only advice I would give myself if I were in your spot . . .That all this has affected your physical condition is not to be wondered at. This siege on top of what you went through a few years ago would be too much for even the most stable individual. From somewhere you must find the strength to fight it. Whatever the cause, whatever its manifestations, the answer lies in fighting, not giving up. Of that I am convinced. The trouble is that I conceive of "fighting" as a sort of ivory-tower self-shut-in-ness, a silent battle raging inside, for the most part unknown to the outside world, showing itself only occasionally when it bursts through, in a rage, or physical symptom of a psychosomatic nature. This has been my conception of "fighting" for many many years now, and it is the kind of fight I have been waging. I suppose I always realized it was a losing battle. Now I know it. And that's the rope I mentioned.

I am so full of tensions, guilts, fears, stresses, strains, cross-purposes, confusions, understandings and lack of understandings, that lately I have been having psychosomatic symptoms—unquestionably psychosomatic. This has done it. Always before this I took a sort of perverted pride in my "strength"—which was really cowardice—in at least managing to keep most of the mess bottled up. But when it breaks out in physical effects, despite my best efforts, I have to recognize the handwriting on the wall. I am no good to Kaye, to the children, to you, or to myself. And I am getting worse. I have slowly been succumbing to a sort of paralysis of the will which finds me, to all intents and purposes, a dead man. Clinically, I am going through what they call a "depression." It's too much, too much for me. I'm taking the fight elsewhere, calling for reinforcements. In a way it's a surrender, in a more important way it's a strategic turn of the battle. I've known all along that I could be helped; there has never been any doubt in my mind about that. But it has been a symptom of my trouble that that very knowledge has stiffened my refusal to face help. Kaye has been after me for a long time to seek it. I have resisted her, too.

Now Sam Yochelson has come out here for a sad business concerning his sister, who is dying of cancer and doesn't know it (or did I write you that?) and because I don't know when I'll see him again I seized the opportunity to ask for help. He is providing it. I don't mean him personally, because that would be impossible both geographically and medically. But he has a colleague here whom he completely trusts and arrangements are being made right now for me to go to this man for psychoanalytic treatment . . . I know, the money. Sam knows my circumstances; I told him. The cost will be minimal. It will take perhaps two years. I must and I will go through with it. And be grateful that I have a friend who is willing and able to help me. If I got physically ill, needing regular weekly treatment, the money would somehow be found for it. Or things sold to pay the bills. I can't let money stand in the way any more. I've used it as an excuse for too long, and meanwhile I have paid out plenty in medical bills for others in my family, both immediate and remote.

Well, that is that and, since I have always understood that once a treatment of this sort starts it must not be discussed with anyone but the analyst, it may well be that I won't be able to tell you much if anything from this point on in. So if I don't refer to this matter again, you'll understand why. I am going into this thing with a heavy heart, an exhausted body, and a completely conflicted personality, and I am hoping that when I come out of it I will be a reasonably "normal" human being, with clarity of mind, an ability to concentrate (which I have all but lost), some sort of efficiency, and a spirit relatively untroubled— capable of facing life as it has to be faced—and certainly not least, of enjoying it. Right now it is a burden and a recrimination. I'm afraid to let myself go on much longer in this way—I use "afraid" literally. I still have some years left to me, I have not provided security for my family, nor have I given them much happiness. They are entitled to both, and if I go on as I have been going they will not only not get either, but they may find me a burden . . . I am not overdramatizing. I am in some sort of crisis which has been gathering itself for a long long time. Obviously, what will affect them will also affect you, although in a different way. Like it or not, we are tied to each other economically and it doesn't look to me as if you and I will ever escape each other. The wise thing to do is obviously to make our association a smooth and cooperative one rather than the angry, sick, inefficient thing it has been and is.

As for your plans. Dan, they are your plans, arising from your pressing problems, and you must do what you feel is best. I am in no condition to evaluate, as I've said. [. . .]

As of this morning, I have some $100 in the bank, of which half has to be taken out to pay the day-woman and for some necessary food, and Monday, when I have to send Betty a check for $70, I shall have to cash in a bond to do it. And there are a few unpaid bills still on my desk.

Ordinarily this situation would have driven me crazy in the past. But I am so sick, so sick and tired, that I can only look at it with a dull, stupid sort of bewilderment. I still haven't had bills for the medical expenses of this past six weeks. Where will I get it when those bills come in? I don't know. I don't know. I can't seem to crawl out from under. All I want to do is crawl in deeper and pull the hole over my head. It is because I feel this way that I am seeking psychiatric help; at least, that is one of the important reasons. I mustn't feel this way and I'll do my best to snap out of it. In the meantime, I must manage as best I can. Recently I have been living from week to week. Now I am living from day to day. I had a generous offer from Sam to lend me some money. Naturally I refused. But it may even come to that. One gets in deeper.[. . .]

I suppose if I added up all the money I have paid to Betty in the past 10 or 11 years, plus the divorce, the law suit expenses, my moving to California, etc., etc., it would even itself up. The drain on me has been steady and remorseless. Kaye and I haven't lived "high"—quite the contrary . . . And how much money have you spent on your short story library? It just beats me.

This is all very incoherent and I'm going to stop it.

* * *

[. . .] I can give you at least something untainted by sickness of spirit, and that's my fervent hope that Stevie is on his way to a healthier state. And my love to Bill, too.

MANNY

March 9, 1950

Dear Man:

[. . .] I know that you and Kaye will be happy to learn that since I last wrote to you, Steve has shown a definite improvement; he has gained weight (all that he lost since the hospital and more); he is standing up again; his personality is improved—he is much more his old happier self. Bill and I are elated, even though we force ourselves to go easy with our hopes—we don't know, of course, whether the improvement will continue. The doctors are flabbergasted, and don't know what to think. It might be the insulin, which we are continuing to give him twice a day. Whatever it is, we hope for the best. Bill's optimism never wavered—she deserves a break. If Steve continues to improve, it will mean a new lease on life for Bill and me. I am no longer the atheistic wise-guy I once was—I haven't been for some time now; I have had too much trouble to remain intellectually self-sufficient; trouble brings even arrogance to its knees, and in my trouble I have learned that I need help, and that the simple, basic beliefs are not so simple and are infinitely basic. I have learned that in my own way I am a much more religious person than I ever dreamed . . .

DAN

Envoi

Dannay's hopes for Stephen went unfulfilled. There was no permanent improvement, and Stephen Dannay died in 1954 at the age of six.

In 1950 Lee and his family returned to the East Coast, eventually settling in Roxbury, Connecticut.

Over the next 20 years, there were certainly more letters; two of them will round out this collection. There were certainly more telephone calls, more territorial disputes, more hotly contested opinions, more books. But we've reached the end of the correspondence contained in the Dannay Papers.

We close with two letters from Lee.

The first was written just before he went into the hospital for heart-related problems—problems that would eventually kill him—and it is filled with physical and emotional pain. The second is part of a note regarding the manuscript that very likely was the cousins' last novel, *A Fine and Private Place*.

Agony and work, those staples of their correspondence, were also the poles of the lives of Dannay and Lee, right to the very end.

April 13, 1962

Dear Dan:

[. . .] I'm not really afraid of dying, Dan. I don't want to die, because I don't have the comfort of believing in the post-existence of the personality after death, and death to me means extinction, obliteration. But what the hell difference does it make to the individual? So you go to sleep, and you don't wake up...With me it's not fear of death *per se*. It's fear, in a sense, of life—consciousness of enormous waste of vital resources and opportunities, of personal failure on a devastating scale, which has unfortunately affected my wife and children, you, and perhaps others.

I'd like to live on so that I may salvage something from the wreckage, bring some order out of the chaos . . . make more sense as a functioning human being before the inevitable comes to pass. When I look back on my life it seems to me almost non-human in content, in the sense that to be human is to achieve, to rise above oneself, to pull out of life a kind of victory against the odds. I have never been happy, I have never had an instant's peace of mind, I have never known unalloyed pride in myself, I've brought so much pain to those I love to outweigh the few joys I've been able to put into the balance . . . It makes me angry to think about it—I mean with myself; and I would like the chance to do what I know I have it in me to do— first for myself, and through myself to others, because it can't be done in any other sequence. [. . .]

As we've both said on occasion, you and I are married to each other; and if more often than not it's felt like a marriage made in hell—on both sides—there it is, and neither of us can do anything about the past third of a century. Don't misunderstand me; I'm not crying *"Mea Culpa!"* to Sir Galahad. We share the guilt; it takes two to make such a marriage; in our respective weaknesses, psychologically, we needed each other, and perhaps we shall continue to need each other so long as both of us live. But it's an unhealthy need, and I for one would like to live long enough to see the relationship cured of its illness and turned into a healthy one. If, by some remote chance, I don't come out of this, I wanted you to know that.

MAN

One thing more. Kaye is under great strain. She pretends not to be worried, but of course she is; and I suppose she will be until I'm out of the hospital and safely back on the dicumeral. You can help her, and me, a great deal by treating this as an ordinary business—not evincing any particular anxiety, etc. They expect to have me on my feet on Wednesday, and there's no reason why you can't call me directly at the hospital—even on Tuesday, for that matter. My best to Bill.

June 19, 1970

Dear Dan:

[. . .] I should have the MS. of the new novel in your hands by the middle of next week.

MAN

The Finishing Stroke

Time has not treated Dannay and Lee well.

Ellery Queen, author and detective, has faded from public consciousness. Mystery critic Marvin Lachman attributes the drop in Queen's stock to nothing less than the decline of Western civilization. He is joking, but there is bitter truth in that joke. This is not a culture that places great value on ratiocination, on cerebral activity. Attention spans have shrunk, spectacle rules, and the paradigm has shifted from *Sleuth* to Uncouth. The quasi-pornography of forensics has supplanted the reasonable consideration of "the facts in the matter." Poirot's little grey cells are only of interest when they are splattered against a wall by a .38-caliber Police Special.

Ellery Queen is the Forgotten Man of the mystery world. All of the books, from the early puzzle-based brain-busters to the last self-reflexive riffs on the EQ canon, are out of print. Ellery hasn't appeared on television since the 1975-76 series on NBC. William Link, who created that series with the late Richard Levinson, believes the show failed because it was too intelligent for most viewers.

Another possible reason for the Queenian eclipse makes for a curious bit of irony. Fred Dannay worked hard to keep Ellery and his adventures up-to-date and responsive to the times. Ellery's character evolved over the years to reflect a changing world and a changing market, with the result that there is no single Ellery for the casual reader to grab on to. To paraphrase Gertrude Stein, Poirot is Poirot is Poirot, but Ellery went through several major incarnations. The mannered, bloodless aesthete of *The Roman Hat Mystery* has almost nothing in common with the conscience-ridden, flesh-and-blood man of *Ten Days' Wonder*. Fans who like the novels from the early years are not always enamored of EQ's later outings, and vice-versa.

As ambitious as Dannay and Lee were within the form, they never trumpeted their importance outside of it. There was no jockeying for position or overt claims to literary significance or sociological distinction, *a la* Raymond Chandler. Respected giants in the field, they were just another pair of mystery writers to the reputation-making critics and scholars—mere entertainers purveying trivialities.

Jon L. Breen has written with great acuity about the disappearance of EQ from general consciousness. Classic fair-play exercises in deduction, Breen says, are considered feminine and British, and therefore the province of Christie, Sayers, Marsh, Allingham, *et alia*. American detective fiction is thought to be the sole domain of the *Black Mask* Boys, Hammett and Chandler and the gang. The American version is hard, cynical, two-fisted. This is a highly simplified view of the genre's history, but it's the dominant one. "The result of this pigeonholing is that American male classicists," Breen writes, "the greatest of whom was Ellery Queen, tend to be marginalized." And, therefore, forgotten.

Breen notes that the prose style of the books is a problem for some readers. Lee's writing does indeed have its excesses, and sometimes his reach exceeded his grasp. But the mature books of the canon are marvelously alive, marvelously gripping, and this is due to Lee's skills as a writer.

Breen points out that writing teams get less respect than individual authors, and summarizes critical response to collaborative efforts: "Two-handed fiction may be good commerce, but how can distinct creative visions combine to achieve the status of art?" The single (and singular) voice is the Romantic ideal that has shaped our perception of the writer. In cork-lined room or cold-water flat, one labors alone. Anything else is hackwork.

Breen also believes that the series of ghostwritten, non-Ellery mysteries from the 1960s and '70s have damaged Dannay and Lee's reputation. There's every reason to agree with him. These are undistinguished titles with little to recommend them. They kept the EQ name in front of the public and put some money in the coffers, but in retrospect these novels are more of a liability than a credit. Because of them, Ellery Queen is perceived by many to be a brand name, a franchise.

Several Ellery novels were planned by Dannay but written by third parties due to Lee's enormous case of writer's block, which lasted from the late 1950s into the middle 1960s. Theodore Sturgeon wrote *The Player on the Other Side* (1963), Avram Davidson wrote *And on the Eighth Day . . .* (1964) and *The Fourth Side of the Triangle* (1965). Lee and Dannay revised all three manuscripts and—as Dannay's two surviving sons Douglas and Richard have argued—they should be thought of as legitimate Queen novels. *House of Brass*, from 1968, is attributed to Sturgeon by some and by others to Davidson. It should also be included in the canon, though it is one of the weaker Queens.

Breen's ultimate reason for the disappearance of EQ corresponds exactly with the opinions of Marvin Lachman and William Link: "Ellery Queen has fallen from public attention because our respect for intelligence, our cultural literacy, and our attention span are all in steep decline."

Given all this, I still remain confident in Ellery Queen's survival. The 1975-76 television series was released on DVD in the fall of 2010. This charming period piece should lead viewers to the books—or, one might say, to the e-books, as several Queen titles are now available digitally. The Internet shows signs of a renewal of interest in Queen; several websites are devoted to EQ, and a great deal of Queenian discussion turns up on mystery-related blogs.

Dannay and Lee's view of the world often approaches the blackness of *noir*, but they will never achieve the sort of bleak sainthood that Cornell Woolrich or David Goodis have been awarded. Ellery may have been plunged into despair on occasion, but the slough of despond was not his final home. He may have been taught in the most painful way that reason and logic are weapons that can be used against him, but he never abandoned them.

What Dannay and Lee have in their favor is the excellence of their work. The best of it is as good as the mystery gets.

Novelty fades; fashions pass; but quality endures. Books as fine as *Ten Days' Wonder*, *Cat of Many Tails* and *The Origin of Evil* will be read, remembered, and recommended to others for a long time to come.

Acknowledgements

Blood Relations would not have been possible without the permission of the Frederic Dannay Literary Property Trust and the Manfred B. Lee Family Literary Property Trust. Trustees Douglas and Richard Dannay and Patricia Lee Caldwell and Rand B. Lee have been most generous with their time and assistance, as has the Trusts' agent Jack Time.

Thanks are due as well to Jennifer Lee, Librarian for Public Services, Rare Book and Manuscript Library, Columbia University in the City of New York, and her knowledgeable and friendly staff.

William Link is not only a master of his craft and a legendary figure in the television and mystery worlds, he is as nice a fellow as one could hope to meet. I am so very pleased he is a part of this book.

Anyone who writes about Dannay, Lee and Ellery Queen is indebted to Francis M. Nevins. *Royal Bloodline*: *Ellery Queen, Author and Detective* is the gold standard of Queen studies. Nevins has definitively framed the way we view Dannay and Lee's work.

Jon L. Breen and Marvin Lachman have also made valuable contributions to Queen studies and deserve every fan's gratitude.

No list of acknowledgements would be complete without a tip of the hat to the friends and colleagues who provided help in one way or another: Eileen Connolly, Michael Connolly, Brenda Copeland, Gordon Dahlquist, Larry Ganem, Barry Jay Kaplan, E. J. McCarthy and Mike Nevins.

Three-and-a-half decades since we first met, Mrs. Patricia Zaborowski remains a source of inspiration.

Joan Schenkar said the right words at the right time.

Marion Christensen has labored quietly in the background for years. Her support and belief in this project—and in so many others—are acknowledged with pleasure.

Honor Molloy has been of supreme help in the assembling, editing and annotating of this volume. A gifted writer, she has taken time away from her own work to help make mine better. She is invaluable in more ways than I can enumerate, and she has my deepest thanks and love.

Photo: Eileen Connolly

About the Editor

Joseph Goodrich is an author and dramatist whose plays have
been produced internationally. *Panic,* published by Samuel
French, received the 2008 Edgar Award for best play. An active
member of the Mystery Writers of America, he is represented in
the MWA anthology *The Rich and the Dead*. His nonfiction has
appeared in *Crimespree* magazine. He lives in Brooklyn, N.Y.

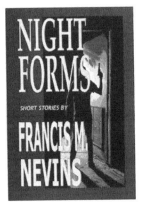
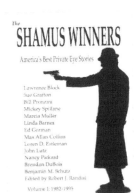

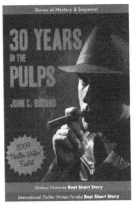

1302028R00082

Made in the USA
San Bernardino, CA
08 December 2012